Literature in the Ashes of History

Literature in the Ashes of History

CATHY CARUTH

Johns Hopkins University Press

Baltimore

Johns Hopkins University Press
2715 North Charles Street
Baltimore, Maryland 21218-4363
www.press.jhu.edu

Library of Congress Cataloging-in-Publication Data
Caruth, Cathy, 1955–
Literature in the ashes of history / Cathy Caruth.
     pages cm
Includes index.
ISBN 978-1-4214-1154-5 (hardcover : acid-free paper) — ISBN 978-1-4214-1155-2
(pbk. : acid-free paper) — ISBN 978-1-4214-1156-9 (electronic) — ISBN 1-4214-1154-7
(hardcover : acid-free paper) — ISBN 1-4214-1155-5 (pbk. : acid-free paper) – ISBN
1-4214-1156-3 (electronic)
   1. Literature and history. 2. Psychic trauma in literature. 3. Collective memory in
literature. I. Title.
PN50.C38   2013
809'.93358—dc23   2013010474

A catalog record for this book is available from the British Library.

*Special discounts are available for bulk purchases of this book. For more information,
please contact Special Sales at 410-516-6936 or specialsales@press.jhu.edu.*

Johns Hopkins University Press uses environmentally friendly book materials, including
recycled text paper that is composed of at least 30 percent post-consumer waste, whenever
possible.

For

Elaine G. Caruth, Ph.D., 1926–1998

and

Clifton J. Caruth, Ph.D., 1925–2002

CONTENTS

At the heart of *Beyond the Pleasure Principle*, as the opening chapter of this book will show, is the striking encounter between an adult and a child: between Sigmund Freud, in the process of attempting to articulate the secrets of the workings of the mind, and the child who plays *"fort"* and *"da"* ("gone" and "here") with a wooden spool on a string that he keeps throwing away and bringing back. The playing child is for the first time facing the absence of his mother, and Freud's interpretation of the game draws the enigmatic sounds of the child's cries into relation with the child's early experience of the departure of the mother that is also, for the small human being facing it, potentially a traumatic loss. Set against the backdrop of World War I and Freud's description of the traumatized soldiers returning from the battlefield, the child's game carries with it a special significance: the pathos of a startled being, bewildered by an inexplicable absence, desperately trying, with each pull of the string, to make the world with which he was familiar reappear. The game of *fort/da,* framed by the losses of the war, thus speaks indirectly to a larger predicament, felt not only by the child, but also by the adult who stands, in perplexity, before him: both are experiencing the looming danger of a world that might vanish, a world that, in its newly unleashed forms of destructiveness, may also be about to disappear.

It is Freud's own struggle to interpret the mysterious (and at first unintelligible) game—a struggle that in many ways unwittingly repeats the recurring gestures of the child's play—that indeed turns this passage, in my reading, into the story of a larger confrontation, that of the encounter of psychoanalysis with a history that cannot simply be assimilated into the theory of repressed desire. What Freud faces in this enigmatic child's game is, I argue, itself a kind of existential and potentially traumatic loss, a loss both of a given psychoanalytic understanding of the child and of a history that could reappear after the work of psychoanalytic understanding has been completed. What comes back with each pull of the string—of the child's game, or of psychoanalytic theory—may not simply be the return of understanding but also the return and disappearance of a history that cannot be exhaustively defined by either consciousness or the acquired theory of psychoanalytic thought. The story of the child's game, as I suggest in various chapters of this book, and as I expand its significance through my readings of the earlier and later Freud, is thus also the story of psychoanalysis itself faced by the threat of a world that is disappearing in the destruction of the two world wars, as well as by the threat of its own disappearing history, a *history of disappearance* that returns in the very gestures of understanding, and of the writing of psychoanalytic theory.

This book will ask: What does it mean for history to disappear? And what does it mean to speak of a history that disappears? These questions lie not only at the center of the psychoanalytic texts in this book but also of the haunting literary narratives of Honoré de Balzac and of Ariel Dorfman, which, in different geographical, historical, linguistic, cultural, and political contexts, recount the traumatic struggles of characters attempting to reappear in the legal and political realms from which they have been banished. In Balzac's story of the return of the Napoleonic soldier Colonel Chabert from the battlefield grave in which he has been buried alive, Balzac draws the unsettling picture of a survivor struggling to come back to life—to reappear both socially and politically in a world that does not recognize him— against the larger background of the repeated emergence and disappearance of revolutionary history in the aftermath of the Napoleonic wars. Similarly, though in the context of a different geography and of a different twentieth-century history, the Chilean American writer Ariel Dorfman delineates, in the story of his central character Paulina—a "disappeared person" who returns to claim justice after the end of a dictatorial regime—the struggle of a woman to reappear in a world to which she no longer belongs, against the background of a political system in the transition to democracy, as it vacillates between the return and disappearance of its own troubled political legacy.

It is the political problem of the emergence and the theoretical articulation of a new history of disappearance that, I argue, likewise drives the innovative historical analysis of Hannah Arendt, whose late essays on lying and politics seek to describe the unfolding of a twentieth-century political history that seems no longer to establish, but rather to eliminate, the very possibility of its own remembrance. From the perspective of Balzac's and Dorfman's powerful and compelling narratives, Hannah Arendt's writing on the "modern lie" may be understood as a rigorous attempt to articulate a new and perplexing phenomenon: the advent of a history that is constituted by the way it disappears from consciousness, that eludes or erases memory in the very act of creating new events. In this sense Arendt's political writing, and Freud's psychoanalytic texts, unwittingly and unexpectedly meet at the site of a disappearance, at the place where history—as modern lie (Arendt), or as death drive (Freud)—seems to move forward through the erasure of its own memory. History emerges—in Arendt and in Freud, as in Balzac and Dorfman—as the performance of its own disappearance. In attempting to portray the movements of this peculiar receding history, these theoretical thinkers also struggle—not unlike the characters in the literary stories—to claim a new mode of conceptual and historical survival in the face of a history that seems constantly about to disappear.

How can we bear witness to such a disappearing history? At the close of this book I examine how both Freud and Jacques Derrida center their analyses of individual memory and collective historical destiny around a story that takes place at a particular burning site, the volcanic explosion of Vesuvius and the burial of ancient Pompeii in the volcano's burning ash, which sets the scene of Wilhelm Jensen's novella *Gradiva: A Pompeiian Fantasy*, a novella that Freud and Derrida read closely. The hero of this story, an archaeologist, also attempts a kind of return, a return to the site of catastrophe to grasp an origin that marks the beginnings of his urgent desire to remember. Both Freud and Derrida turn to this story to trace the steps of this longing for memory and of this return in their own attempts to understand the origins of psychoanalysis and of conceptual thought, but they encounter instead, along with the archaeologist, a ghostly figure who augurs a future burning beyond their imagination of Pompeii or of the conceptual systems of psychoanalysis and of philosophy. At the dawn of the twentieth century, and at its close, each of these profound thinkers thus traces the movement of a burning memory—a burning for memory as well as its burning up—at the heart of a steadily vanishing history. The disappearance of memory—its reenacted obliteration and its literal burning-up in the wars of the early twentieth century—will reemerge, in its own ghostly way, in the psychoanalytic and philosophical writings of these two great thinkers of the era of historical catastrophe.

At the site of this disappearance, however, we can recognize the persistence of a language, or a writing, that emerges precisely as the archival resources of meaning and tradition slip away. It is the language of the life drive, I suggest in the opening chapter of this book, by which Freud signals a mode of speaking and of writing that bear witness to the past by turning toward the future. From the perspective of my final chapter—separated from the first by a profound political disruption in the United States, and by the opening decade of a new, already deeply troubled, century—this language of life must be reread, and understood anew, through the losses, and disappearances, of an era in which the very possibility of the future is fundamentally in doubt. What does it mean to make a claim to life in the face of this disappearing world? This would also be the challenge for the theory of trauma, I would argue, as it passes on its own languages of death and survival into the new, and changing, dangers of the twenty-first century. And it is the burning question that passes from the language of life that begins this book to the psychoanalytic, theoretical, and literary writing that emerges, in and on the ashes, in its final pages.

ACKNOWLEDGMENTS

I would like to thank my Emory students for more than sixteen years of inspired class discussion, conversation, and research. Their voices can be heard in every chapter of this book. I would also like to thank my new students at Cornell for their vibrant contributions and research. I am particularly grateful for the excellent research assistance of Brian McGrath, Luke Donahue (who also provided the index), Jennifer Orth, Armando Mastrogiovanni, Ronald Mendoza de Jesus, Gustavo Llarull, Avery Slater, and Emily Clark, who worked with great care and diligence on the final manuscript.

My intellectual encounters with Elizabeth Rottenberg and Shoshana Felman are the sustaining and inspiring center of my creative life, and I am deeply grateful to both of them for sharing their brilliance and incisive analyses and for their critical attentiveness to my work. I would also like to thank Michal Shaked for introducing me to the Balzac novella and for her profound insight into this remarkable book. Cynthia Chase has been a continuing model of intellectual rigor and originality and has offered crucial comments on my work.

I cannot begin to give an adequate account of the personal and intellectual significance for me of my outstanding colleagues at Emory, as well as my new colleagues at Cornell, and of my friends, students, and audiences at other universities all over the world who, over the years, have meant so much to me in providing venues for developing ideas and who affirm the possibilities of intellectual survival in our challenged era. Their particular contributions are acknowledged in the notes of each chapter. Of these colleagues and friends, Hannah Wojciehowski has provided ongoing critical responses and support, for which I am deeply grateful. Peggy Phelan, Kevin Newmark, Jill Robbins, and Diana Fuss have been important sources of stimulating dialogue and exchange. Jonathan Culler, Thomas Keenan, Dalia Judovitz, Elissa Marder, Claire Nouvet, Deborah White, Rick Rambuss, Ralph Freedman, Nadine Kaslow, Francoise Davoine, Jean-Max Gaudillière, and Nina Goldin have also remained particularly significant interlocutors and supporters. I would also like to thank John Raymond and

Mary Lou Kenney for their patient and thoughtful copyediting and preparation of the text.

I acknowledge permission from the following journals and publishers:

An earlier version of chapter one appeared in *Cultural Values* (now *Journal for Cultural Research*), special issue on Testimonial Cultures, ed. Jackie Stacey, 5, no. 1 (January 2001).

An earlier version of chapter two appeared as "The Claims of the Dead: Trauma, Haunted Property, and the Law," in *Critical Inquiry* 28, no. 2 (Winter 2002).

An earlier version of chapter three appeared in *Arendt in Dark Times*, ed. Roger Berkowitz and Thomas Keenan (Fordham University Press, 2009).

PART ONE

Literature and the Life Drive

CHAPTER ONE

Parting Words

TRAUMA, SILENCE, AND SURVIVAL

Sigmund Freud, *Beyond the Pleasure Principle*

[*For Elaine G. Caruth, Ph.D.**]

TOWARD THE BEGINNING of his groundbreaking work *Beyond the Pleasure Principle*, Sigmund Freud writes of his astonished encounter with the veterans of World War I, whose dreams of the battlefield bring them back, repeatedly, to the horrifying scenes of death that they have witnessed. Like the victims of accident neuroses, these dreams seem to bring the soldiers back to a moment of fright or surprise that constituted their original encounter with death: "Now dreams occurring in traumatic neuroses have the characteristic of repeatedly bringing the patient back into the situation of his accident, a situation from which he wakes up in another fright. This astonishes people far too little" (13).[1] The repetition of battlefield horrors in the dreams astonishes Freud, because dreams, in psychoanalytic theory, had always served the function of fulfilling wishes: of allowing the unconscious, conflictual desires of childhood to find expression through the symbolic world of the dream.

In the dreams of the returning veterans, however, the encounter with death and horror cannot be assimilated to the fulfillment of desire: rather than turning into a symbol or vehicle of psychic meaning, these traumatic dreams seem to turn the psyche itself into the vehicle for expressing the terrifying literality of a history it does not completely own. But the peculiarity of this returning, literal history also strikes Freud because it does not only bring back the reality of death but the fright or unpreparedness for it: the

*I dedicate this chapter to my mother, Elaine G. Caruth, a psychoanalyst who worked for many years with children and adolescents and later with adults. She had discussed an earlier version of this text with me a number of times before her death in March 1998.

dreams not only show the scenes of battle but wake the dreamer up in another fright. Freud's surprised encounter with the repetitive dreams of war—the beginning of the theory of trauma, and of history, that has become so central to our contemporary thinking about history and memory—thus raises the urgent and unavoidable questions: *What does it mean for the reality of war to appear in the fiction of the dream? What does it mean for life to bear witness to death? And what is the surprise that is encountered in this witness?*

Immediately after discussing the disturbing dreams of the war, however, Freud proposes to "leave the dark and dismal subject of the traumatic neurosis" and to pass on to the "normal" activity of child's play. Freud embarks here upon a story of his encounter with another repetitive behavior, the "puzzling activity" of a "good little boy" of one and a half, just beginning to speak. Freud says he observed the strange game of this child who repeatedly threw a wooden spool on a string into his cot, uttering the sound "o-o-o-o," then retrieved it, uttering "a-a-a-a." With the help of the boy's mother, Freud first interprets these encounters as meaning *fort*, "gone," and *da*, "here," and ultimately suggests that the child is reenacting the departure and return of his mother, which he had just been forced to confront. The repetitive game, as a story, thus seems to represent the inner symbolic world of the child: as a story of departure and return, the game seems not only symbolically to fulfill a wish by telling the story of the mother's departure as the story of her return but also to substitute, for the pain of loss, the very pleasure of creation itself.[2] But Freud himself unexpectedly proceeds to challenge his own first interpretation:

> Our interest is directed to another point. The child cannot possibly have felt his mother's departure as something agreeable or even indifferent. . . . It may perhaps be said in reply that her departure had to be enacted as a necessary preliminary to her joyful return, and that it was in the latter that lay the true purpose of the game. But against this must be counted the observed fact that the first act, that of departure, was staged as a game in itself and far more frequently than the episode in its entirety, with its pleasurable ending. (15–16)

The creative activity of the child's game, Freud recognizes with surprise, does not ultimately involve a symbolic representation of the mother's pleasurable return, but repeats, in a kind of stammer that interrupts its story, the painful memory of her departure. Like the soldiers' dreams, the game thus reenacts the memory of a painful reality. What is most surprising in the child's game, however, is that this reenactment of reality in the game places repetition at the very heart of childhood, and links the repetition to a creative act of invention. In the introduction of the child's game, Freud's original question, *what does it mean for life to bear witness to death?*, is thus linked to another question: *What kind of witness is a creative act?*

I will propose in what follows that Freud's insight into trauma in *Beyond the Pleasure Principle*, his new understanding of personal and of collective history in the face of war, lies precisely in the striking and enigmatic leap that juxtaposes the nightmares of war to the child's game. This juxtaposition is not ordinarily taken into account in the critical reception of Freud's text—the study of trauma in contemporary fields tends to focus on a theory of history and memory derived ultimately from the example of the nightmare and the theory that grows out of it, and the writing on the child's game is not part of the tradition of trauma theory[3]—but it is crucial, I will suggest, for understanding the insight of Freud. My own understanding of this insight did not emerge, however, simply through a reading of Freud's text but began, in fact, in my encounter with a real child in Atlanta, a child whose best friend was murdered in the street and who is interviewed by the friend's mother. By reading together the language of the nightmare and the language of the child in Freud's text—two very distinct kinds of language whose intertwining strands are at the heart of Freud's theory—and in then understanding how Freud's text and the language of the real child shed light upon each other, we can begin to understand Freud's enigmatic move in the theory of trauma from the drive for death to the drive for life, from the reformulating of life around the witness to death to the possibility of witnessing and making history in creative acts of life.

DEATH AND AWAKENING

Freud's analysis of repetition compulsion in the origins of consciousness attempts to explain the significance and surprise of the traumatic encounter with death in terms of a new relation between consciousness and life.[4] Consciousness first arose, Freud speculates, as an attempt to protect the life of the organism from the imposing stimuli of a hostile world, by bringing to its attention the nature and direction of external stimuli. The protective function of consciousness as taking in bits of the world, however, was less important, Freud suggests, than its more profound function of keeping the world out, a function it accomplished by placing stimuli in an ordered experience of time. What causes trauma, then, is an encounter that is not directly perceived as a threat to the life of the organism but that occurs, rather, as a break in the mind's experience of time: "We may, I think, tentatively venture to regard the common traumatic neurosis as a consequence of an extensive breach being made in the protective shield against stimuli. . . . We still attribute importance to the element of fright. It is caused by lack of any pre-paredness for anxiety" (31). The breach in the mind—the psyche's aware-ness of the threat to life—is not caused by a direct threat or injury, but by fright, the lack of preparedness to take in a stimulus that comes too quickly. It is not the direct perception of danger, that is, that constitutes the threat for the psyche, but the fact that the danger is recognized as such one mo-ment too late. It is this lack of direct experience that thus becomes the basis of the repetition of the traumatic nightmare: "These dreams are endeavor-ing to master the stimulus retrospectively, by developing the anxiety whose omission was the cause of the traumatic neurosis" (32). The return of the traumatic experience is not the direct witness of a threat to life but rather the attempt to overcome the fact that it was not direct, to master what was never fully grasped in the first place. And since consciousness cannot bear witness to death, the life of the survivor becomes the repetition of the reality that consciousness cannot grasp. In the traumatic encounter with death, life itself attempts to serve as the witness that consciousness cannot provide.

The repetition exemplified by the nightmare, we might note in this con-text, does not only concern the repetition of the image in the dream, but also, as I have suggested elsewhere, the repetition of waking from it: "Dreams occurring in traumatic neuroses have the characteristic of repeatedly bring-ing the patient back into the situation of his accident, a situation from which he *wakes up in another fright*" (13, my emphasis).[5] If "fright" is the term by which Freud defines the traumatic effect of not having been prepared in time, then the trauma of the nightmare does not simply consist in the experience within the dream but in the experience of waking from it. It is the surprise of waking that repeats the unexpectedness of the trauma. And as such the trauma is not only the repetition of the missed encounter with death but also the missed encounter with one's own survival. It is the incomprehensible act of surviving—of waking into life—that repeats and bears witness to what remains ungrasped within the encounter with death.

The repetition of trauma, therefore, is not only an attempt or an impera-tive to know what cannot be grasped that is repeated unconsciously in the survivor's life; it is also an *imperative to live* that still remains not fully un-derstood. And it is this incomprehensible imperative to live that Freud ulti-mately places at the very origin of life, when he suggests that life itself began as the drive to death: "The attributes of life were at some time awoken in inanimate matter by the action of a force of whose nature we can form no conception. . . . The tension which then arose in what had hitherto been an inanimate substance endeavored to cancel itself out. In this way the first drive came into being: the drive to return to the inanimate state" (38, translation modified).

Life originates, Freud here suggests, as an awakening from "death" for which there was no preparation. Life itself, that is, is an imperative to awaken that precedes any understanding or consciousness and any possible desire or wish.[6] The witness of survival itself—the awakening that constitutes life—lies not only in the incomprehensible repetition of the past, but in the incomprehensibility of a future that is not yet owned. Freud's central question raised by the nightmare, *what does it mean for life to bear witness to death?*, thus ultimately leads to another, more urgent and enigmatic question: *In what way is the experience of trauma also the experience of an imperative to live? What is the nature of a life that continues beyond trauma?*

THE CHILD'S GAME

From one perspective, Freud's analysis can be understood as having replaced the notion of the child, and its central place in psychoanalytic theory, with the theory of trauma. The child's repetition of its mother's departure could be explained as the unknowing reliving of its mother's (anticipated) death, and the child's life as the unconscious reliving of what is not yet grasped within the mother's departure. From the perspective of Freud's rethinking of life around its traumatic significance, the child's game thus peculiarly reenacts the incomprehensible moment of the mother's act of leaving and reshapes the very life of the child as the unconscious witness to the death he has survived. Repeating the *fort* that is not his own but his mother's act of leaving, the child's own life story—his departure into life—becomes inextricable from his mother's silent departure into death. In this incomprehensible departure, the child's life—like the origin of the drive—thus silently enacts a larger history he does not completely own.[7]

Freud's analysis suggests, indeed, that the encounter with traumatic repetition requires a rethinking of psychoanalysis itself, which had previously focused its model of the mind on the notion of childhood as the site of the pleasure principle. By modeling the mind on the encounter with war trauma, Freud appears to shift the center of psychoanalytic thinking from the individual struggle with internal Oedipal conflicts of childhood to the external, collective activities of history, and to make of childhood a reflection of a more obscure and painful encounter. Thus Robert Jay Lifton writes that the reversal of adult and child trauma as a model for the human mind was at the center of *Beyond the Pleasure Principle*, and produced the "image-model of the human being as a perpetual survivor."[8] The questions raised by war trauma concerning the nature of life thus require a new model for psycho-analytic thinking and, in particular, for the relation between psychoanalysis and history.

BEGINNING AGAIN

Yet the game of the child playing *fort* and *da*, gone and here, with his spool seems to become not less, but more, enigmatic when it is understood in relation to traumatic repetition. If the child's reenactment of his mother's departure repeats, ultimately, her loss and her death, the game remains, nonetheless, an act of creation that, unlike the dream of the war veterans, does not simply compulsively repeat a history it doesn't own but creates, in its repetition, something new.[9] This very movement from the example of traumatic repetition in the war nightmare to the example of the child will, moreover, reappear surprisingly in Freud's text, and will reappear precisely at the moment that Freud has explained the notion of trauma in the origin of life. For shortly after introducing the origin of life as an awakening out of death, Freud pauses abruptly and starts again:

> But let us pause for a moment and reflect. It cannot be so. The sexual instincts, to which the theory of the neuroses gives a quite special place, appear under a very different aspect. . . . The whole path of development to natural death is not trodden by *all* the elementary entities which compose the complicated body of one of the higher organisms. Some of them, the germ cells, probably retain the original structure of living matter and, after a certain time . . . separate themselves from the organism as a whole. . . . Under favourable conditions, they begin to develop—that is, to repeat the performance [*das Spiel wiederholen*] to which they owe their existence; and in the end once again one portion of their substance pursues its development to a finish, while another portion harks back once again as a fresh residual germ to the beginning of the process of development. . . . They are the true life drives. (39–40, translation modified)

The origin of life as the death drive—as the beginning of the repetition compulsion, and as an awakening—is itself repeated, Freud audaciously suggests, and is repeated, moreover, precisely in the form of a game (*Spiel*). After disappearing for most of his text since his original introduction of the child—and disappearing in particular from the theory of trauma, which is entirely governed by the language of consciousness and awakening[10]—the language of the game reappears, and reappears to describe a different form of repetition: a repeating of the origin of life in another kind of beginning.[11] This repetition brings back, moreover, for the very first time, the explicit language of the child's game, the language Freud uses at the moment he recognizes the game as a game of departure: "But against this must be counted the observed fact that the first act, that of departure, was staged as a game in itself and far more frequently than the episode in its entirety, with its pleasurable ending" [*daß der erste Akt, das Fortgehen, für sich allein als Spiel inszeniert wurde, und zwar ungleich häufiger als das zum lustvollen Ende fortgeführte Ganze*] (16). This game, and the event of departure that it re-enacts, is now repeated as the very action of the life drive: "Under favourable conditions, they begin to develop—that is, to repeat the performance to which they owe their existence; and in the end once again one portion of their substance pursues its development to a finish" [*Unter günstige Bedingungen gebracht, beginnen sie sich zu entwickeln, das heißt das Spiel, dem sie ihre Entstehung verdanken, zu wiederholen, und dies endet damit, daß wieder ein Anteil ihrer Substanz die Entwicklung bis zum Ende fortführt*] (40). Freud thus reintroduces the language of departure not as the origin of the death drive, but as the way it repeats itself, differently, as the drive for life.[12] The departure into life is not simply the awakening that repeats an original death, but an act of parting that distinguishes, precisely, between death and life.[13] The occurrence of this game then, as an origin, is the beginning of life as a surprising repetition that both bears witness to and breaks from the death drive, that bears witness and repeats by precisely breaking away. It is a language of departure, that is, that does not repeat the unconscious origin of life as death, but creates a history by precisely departing toward survival.

This creative act takes place, moreover, not only at the origin of life and in the child's game, but in Freud's own text, as well, through the very transformation undergone by the language of trauma: from the departure—the *fort*—that appears to be the repetition of the mother's anticipated death in the child's game, to the *fortführen* of the drive that is the pressure toward life.[14] This transformation also differentiates or parts the traumatized subject, the soldiers of war repeating death, from the individual testimony of Freud's own text, the creative act of language that becomes not only the story of departure but also the language of play, a language that would, in fact, become a new language for psychoanalysis in the future. In the life drive, then, life itself, and the language of creativity, begin as an act that bears witness to the past even by turning from it; that bears witness to death by bearing witness to the possibility of origination in life. History, here, is reclaimed and generated not in reliving unconsciously the death of the past but by an act that bears witness by parting from it. The language of the life drive does not simply point backward, that is, but bears witness to the past by pointing to the future. The return of the child's language in *Beyond the Pleasure Principle* thus transforms the original questions of trauma—*what does it mean for life to bear witness to death?* and *what is the nature of a life that continues beyond trauma?*—into an ultimately more fundamental and elusive concern: *What is the language of the life drive?*

MEMENTOS

The significance of this question first arose, for me, not from within Freud's theoretical text, nor in the history of World War I, but in my own encounter with a child in Atlanta, within the contemporary history of urban violence in America. I encountered this child shortly after leaving New Haven and arriving in Atlanta, when I became familiar with a group established in Atlanta to help traumatized children who had witnessed violence, a group called Kids Alive and Loved. This group was established by a woman named Bernadette Leite, whose oldest son, Khalil, was shot in the back and killed one night when he was out with friends, shortly before graduating from high school. The impulse for the group came specifically, as she tells us, not only from witnessing the symptoms of anger and the violent reenactment of trauma in the kids' responses to the death at the funeral and afterward, but when the mother of the dead boy, Bernadette, overheard the peculiar language of children: "After his death I noticed that his friends were coming over every afternoon and hanging out in his room. And I began to listen, and I heard them speaking to him. They would come over every afternoon and hang out in his room and speak to him. And I realized that they needed someone to talk to."[15] Hearing the language of the children addressed only to her dead son, Bernadette recognized the unresolved trauma of many of his friends in their inability to speak about their feelings to the living. She thus decided to found a group to allow children to talk about their feelings to each other concerning the violence they had experienced, in weekly Wednesday night meetings and through videotaped interviews she has made for the Kids Alive and Loved Oral History Archive. Giving the group the name Kids Alive and Loved, whose initials—KAL—reproduce the initials of her child, Khalil Aseem Leite, Bernadette hoped to make the group not only a means of helping the living children to get over their trauma by talking about Khalil (as well as other murders they had experienced) but also of providing a kind of living memorial to her dead son through the living children's words and lives.

The complexity of this process was most movingly portrayed for me, however, through the words of a single child, in the recorded interview of Bernadette with Gregory, Khalil's best friend. Gregory was 17 at the time of his friend's death. He had received a call from Khalil that morning to go out that evening, but argued about being called so early, and then was not at home when he was called again.[16] Gregory speaks, throughout the interview, in a language that tries to convey the difficulty of grasping Khalil's death: when asked to say something about Khalil's life he answers, "He lived for everything. He died for nothing." This inability to grasp the meaning of his friend's death resonates in his own difficulty in extricating a description of Khalil's life from his own survival of Khalil's death:

B: What do you want people to know about his life?
G: He had a good heart.

B: What does [the experience of Khalil's death] feel like?
G: It's like when somebody is actually pulling your heart out, or just repeatedly stabbing it.

The dead Khalil's life and Greg's survival of it are tied around a heart that they share and that has now been removed. Greg's heart, it would appear, being removed and stabbed, tells the story of Khalil's death. In the exchange between Bernadette and Greg, we see Bernadette's attempt to help Greg memorialize Khalil in a kind of language of memory, and we witness Greg's own transformation of her language of memory into a parting that allows for both a memorialization of his friend and a recognition of his own life.

PARTING WORDS

This possibility opens up, strikingly, in a moment of surprise, in a remarkable moment of his interview with her, just at the place moreover, when the interview turns to the topic of memorialization. Bernadette has been asking about Gregory's feelings concerning Khalil's death, and the interview has become very somber and at times filled with sorrow. Then Greg makes the interview take a sudden turn:

B: Do you have any mementos of Khalil?
G: Let's see . . .
B: Do you have personal belongings of his?
G: [suddenly smiling]: He has something of mine!
B: [laughing]: I know he has something of yours . . . a couple of things!
G: He had . . . That's what also made me feel good, because he was buried in my shirt that I loved, and my watch. At first that shirt bothered me because I loved that shirt—
B: And I didn't know at the time. . . . Mark picked it out and I only found out later. It's too bad—I wanted to get him a Tommy Hilfiger shirt he'd

seen downtown but I didn't have time to get it and get to the funeral parlor. It's too bad—but then maybe he wouldn't have been buried in your favorite shirt.

G: That's OK, because it was my favorite shirt and my favorite friend.

Greg's first response to Bernadette's question—"Do you have any personal belongings of his?"—comes as a surprise because it reverses the order by which the living Greg would memorialize his dead friend and suggests that it is the dead friend that is keeping mementos of him: "He has something of mine!" Greg says. This is also, in its irony and humor, a kind of maintenance of the playful relationship that Greg had with the living Khalil: the implicit joke that Khalil got away with his favorite shirt seems to re-create the humorous relationship they had when Khalil was alive. Greg thus, in effect, says "gone!" to his shirt and, in so doing, establishes a relationship with Khalil that recognizes, even within the fiction of personification, the ineradicable difference between his life and Khalil's death.

Bernadette's response, likewise, turns both to the dead and to the living at once, although in a somewhat different fashion. On the one hand she tells, very movingly, of a mother who wants to get one last gift for her dead son, to buy him the shirt that he had seen and wanted. But the telling of this story is simultaneously, and equally movingly, a kind of playful mothering of the living boy in front of her, because she empathizes with him that it is too bad that he could not have had his favorite shirt back. To Gregory's "*fort*!" or "gone!" Bernadette thus says, in effect, "*da*!" or "here!" and, in this way, makes her act of mothering the living boy a continuation of her mothering of the dead one, and makes of Greg the living memory of the dead Khalil.

It is thus particularly striking that Greg's final words, which are the true climax of the exchange for me, once again give up the shirt to Khalil: "That's OK. It was my favorite shirt and my favorite friend." If his first response brought Khalil to life as a youthful friend—and reanimated Greg too as he was before he had the horrible knowledge of Khalil's death—this final response, in giving the gift to Khalil, gives up that former innocence and re-creates Greg through his ability to give to and thus memorialize his dead friend. By once again saying "gone!," Greg indeed departs from his former self and thus turns the memento—and the language of the memento—into an act, not of a symbolic return or wish for possession, but of an ability to give to the dead something that can never, now, be returned.[17]

This double act is repeated, a few minutes later, in the next exchange, an exchange that now, significantly, concerns a game:

B: So it made you feel good that your favorite friend was buried in your favorite shirt and your watch?

G: [Smiling again]: And he has my—it's not really a hat, it's a cap. It's a little like a stocking cap, that colorful thing on his wall. Yeah, him and me and Maurice would play this game, "left hand," where you call out what's in a person's left hand and you get to keep it. And he called that and he got it.

B: I should give that back to you, you could take it with you as a memento.

G: Uh-uh, I would feel better if it would stay in his household. Because it's a memento of him but it's a memento of me too.

The game with his friend, Greg tells us, had been a game of naming and possessing; by calling out the other's clothing it could become yours, just as the friendship was perhaps a kind of reciprocal possession of each boy by the other. But when Bernadette offers, once again, to give the possession back— "I should give it back to you, you could take it with you as a memento"— Greg once again repeats his *fort*: "I would feel better if it would stay in his household. Because it is a memento of him but it's a memento of me too." Naming the cap as a memento not only of Khalil but of himself, Greg not only gives up the part of himself that existed before Khalil's death, he also ties his life with Khalil's death: the cap is not only a memento of him for me, he says, but of me for him. This bond, however, does not confuse the living child with the dead one, nor does it symbolize the dead one in the living one, but precisely separates Greg, whose younger self is buried in the coffin, from the dead child who will not grow past this moment. Indeed, this refusal of Bernadette's offer to give the cap back is also (as my own mother pointed out to me) a way of saying "I will not be your dead child." In giving up the language of memorialization offered by Bernadette, however, he creatively transforms the language of the memento and achieves another language and another memorialization: a memorialization that takes place precisely through his separation and his own act of creation.[18] It is in this reclaiming of the meaning of the memento, even while giving it up, that Greg's *fort*, I would suggest, does not simply reenact his friend's departure or attempt to return to his life, but bears witness, creatively, in the very act of parting from his dead friend.

This language, I would suggest, is the language of the life drive. It is this drive for life that is at work in Greg's description of how the death of his friend is also motivating him to achieve goals in his life, achievements that will also incorporate Khalil's name:

B: How has his death changed your life?

G: I am more determined to make it in the music business somehow and I know it will be because of him. We used to talk about it all the time. He did rap. . . . [W]e were to go to Clark [University], Atlanta, him for business management and me for communication, music, and combine our talents. But now he can't do that. . . . But that's OK, because when I do it I'll bring all the people jobs, Mike, Maurice. . . . When we get that studio [Khalil's] name is going to be the name of it. And I have to have a son and his name will be in there.

In this language we can see the drive for life, a language of parting that itself moves the speaker forward to a life that is not simply possessed, but given, in some sense, and received, as a gift from the dead. In the memento, as Greg teaches us, the two children take leave from each other: as Greg gives Khalil back to death, Khalil, in a sense, gives Greg back to life. This is a creative act, an act that bears witness to the dead precisely in the process of turning away. It is indeed a new language of departure, parting words that bind the living child to the dead one even as he takes leave from him, that bind him to his dead friend even in the very act of letting go.[19]

FREUD'S GAME

In Greg's words, we see the insight of Freud's text as it touches on and resonates with our contemporary crises and with the actual struggles of children in contemporary culture. But Greg's words also shed light on the way in which the language of the child itself reemerges at the heart of Freud's own theoretical writing.[20] For Freud's elaborate staging of the game of the *fort/da* can be understood not only as a description of the puzzling game of the child staging the departure and return of the mother but also as Freud's own oscillation in his understanding of the child's game. This oscillation takes the form, moreover, of the alternation between a *fort* and a *da*:

I eventually realized that it was a game and that the only use he made of any of his toys was to play "gone" with them. (15)

This, then, was the complete game—disappearance and return. As a rule one witnessed only its first act, which was repeated untiringly as a game in itself, though there is no doubt that the greater pleasure was attached to the second act. (15)

It may perhaps be said . . . that [the mother's] departure had to be enacted as a necessary preliminary to her joyful return, and that it was in the latter that lay the true purpose of the game. But against this must be counted the observed fact that the first act, that of departure, was staged as a game in itself and far more frequently than the episode in its entirety, with its pleasurable ending. (15–16)

As Freud's interpretation passes from the *fort* to the narrative of *fort and da* and back again to the *fort*, Freud shows himself struggling in the face of a child whose language, in its shifting meaning for Freud, first brings him nearer and then distances him in Freud's understanding.[21] What is striking in Freud's example, that is, is not simply the child's struggle and reenactment of the distance of its mother, but Freud's struggle with and reenactment of the distance of the child. Freud's text, it would appear, repeats the story of the child he has encountered, and does so, moreover, in the very act of distancing. Paradoxically, then, it will be in his repetition of the child's distance, in his own distancing of the child at the moment of his failed comprehension of the game, that Freud's own text will connect with, and transmit, the story the child cannot quite tell. Freud's text, that is, itself repeats the child's traumatized *fort*—the stammering word that marks the very loss of the child's own story—but does so as the creation of its own new language, a language that does not return to the pleasurable compensations of the narrative but speaks, precisely, from *beyond the story*. It is not necessarily on the level of the child's own game, that is, but on the level of Freud's repetition of it that the creative act of the game, the new conceptual language of the life drive, will take place.[22]

We could, moreover, understand the entire theory of trauma in *Beyond the Pleasure Principle* not simply as an explanation of trauma from the distance of theoretical speculation but as the passage of the story of the child in a theoretical act of transformation.[23] For what is the story of the mind's attempt to master the event retrospectively if not the story of a failed return: the attempt, and failure, of the mind to return to the moment of the event? The theory of repetition compulsion as the unexpected encounter with an event that the mind misses and then repeatedly attempts to grasp is the story of a failure of the mind to return to an experience it has never quite grasped, the repetition of an originary departure from the moment that constitutes the very experience of trauma. And this story appears again as the beginning of life in the death drive, as life's attempt to return to inanimate matter that ultimately fails and departs into a human history.[24] Freud's own theory, then, does not simply describe the death drive and its enigmatic move to the drive for life but enacts this drive for life as the very language of the child that encounters, and attempts to grasp, the catastrophes of a traumatic history.

The most striking appearance of Freud's own speaking as the child will occur, however, not within the theoretical language of the text, but in a footnote that refers, in fact, to the entrance of a real death into the life of the child as well as into his own life: "When this child was five and three-quarters, his mother died. Now that she was really 'gone' ('o-o-o'), the child showed no signs of grief." In noting the real death of the child's mother, Freud first explicitly links the child to himself, since the child's mother was also, in reality, Freud's daughter Sophie, who died toward the end of the writing of *Beyond the Pleasure Principle*. But whereas the (already trauma-tized) child shows no signs of grief, Freud himself begins to repeat, not simply the language of the *fort*, but the inarticulate sounds of the "o-o-o-o" that constituted the origin of the game (and the only moment in which the living mother had appeared in the example, when she agreed with Freud as to the meaning of the "o-o-o-o" as indicating the word *fort*). By reintroduc-ing the lost "o-o-o-o" of the original child's game in his words, and in this footnote that announces his daughter's and the mother's real death, Freud implicitly connects the origin of the child's game with the significance of his own theoretical text, a significance that now, in its inarticulate stammer, serves as a kind of memory of, and parting from, Freud's own dead child.[25] The language of the theory, much like the child's stammering language, ar-ticulates the very notions of trauma and of the death drive as a creative act of parting: a parting from the real child, and a parting from the psychoana-lytic child—or from the mere psychoanalysis of childhood—toward an anal-ysis of collective catastrophes of death encountered in war, and toward the pressing cultural imperative for a new kind of survival.[26]

I would propose that it is through the child's words—through this liter-ary, not fully articulated language of theory—that Freud's text speaks, more-over, most powerfully, in its full historical relevance, to us. For it is through the child's own stammer—the stammer of Freud as he faces the encounter with World War I, the reduction of the theoretical mind to the stammering struggle of the child—that Freud will first tell us about the necessity of wit-nessing the effects of death in the century of trauma. But it is also through the creative transformation of this stammer into a new language of psycho-analysis—not only the language of departure, which will be his language of history in *Moses and Monotheism*, but the future language of psychoanaly-sis itself, in the rethinking of psychoanalysis, for example, around the indi-vidual's capacity for play—that the possibilities of Freud's not yet articulated insight are handed over to us.[27] I would suggest that it is only in listening to this second and literarily creative element in Freud's own writing that the theory of trauma, now so prevalent in numerous disciplines, can extend itself beyond the theory of repetition and catastrophe, beyond the insight of the death drive, into the insight enigmatically passed on in the new notion of the drive to life. As such the theory of trauma does not limit itself to a theoretical formulation of the centrality of death in culture, but constitutes—in Freud's, and our own, historical experience of modernity—an act of parting that itself creates and passes on a different history of survival.

CHAPTER TWO

The Claims of the Dead

HISTORY, HAUNTED PROPERTY, AND THE LAW

Honoré de Balzac, *Colonel Chabert*

H ONORÉ DE BALZAC'S NOVEL, *Colonel Chabert*, first published in 1832, opens with a peculiar scene: a soldier who is known to have died in battle most improbably and unexpectedly returns to the office of a lawyer to reclaim his property. Disfigured and unrecognizable, the stranger insists that he is actually the famous colonel and asks the lawyer to help him to obtain a form of legal recognition that will restore to him his lawful identity, his property, and his wife. In this strange reincarnation of his own dead self, the character appealing to the lawyer hopes to become legally, and therefore humanly, alive. Unfolding from this haunting encounter, Balzac's story dramatizes the attempt by a man who is legally dead to come alive before the law and the capacity and limits of the law to respond to this attempt at legal resuscitation.

Set in post-Revolutionary France during the Restoration, this ghostly return of a Napoleonic soldier clearly echoes the historic repetitions that were taking place during this period: the return to the pre-Revolutionary past during the Restoration, itself ruptured by the return of Napoleon during the 100 Days; the protracted waves of revolutionary socioeconomic shocks to France in the wake of the French Revolution. What is remarkable in Balzac's text is the singular perception that this haunted repetition, this return, takes place not simply in the realm of history, politics, or war, but rather and specifically on the site of the law. What is at stake in Balzac's novel is a legal claim that turns the law itself into the place par excellence of historical memory. This appeal to memory and history through the law emerges in Balzac, moreover, not simply through the return of a living revolutionary hero but, far more unexpectedly and enigmatically, through a return of the dead. What does it mean, Balzac's text seems to ask, for the dead to speak—and to speak before the law? And what does it mean, moreover, for the law to listen to this claim, which is coming, as it were, from the dead? It is through these unsettling questions, I will argue, that Balzac reflects on the complexity of the relationship that, in the wake of the French Revolution, emerges as an entanglement and as an indissoluble bond between the law and history.

It is not by chance, I will suggest, that this literary story takes place as a scene of haunted memory. I will argue that in giving center stage to the return of the dead and to the singular encounter between the survivor and the law, Balzac's text grasps the core of a past and of a future legal haunting and identifies as central to historical development a question of death and of survival. This question will indeed return to haunt the twentieth century, not simply in the central role of Holocaust survivors in the postwar war crime trials but, even more uncannily, in the current legal claims made by individual survivors for restitution of their past property, and, more fundamentally, for restitution of their property rights. Through its strange tale of a ghostly claim to property, Balzac's text thus prophetically conveys, I would propose, what it means for the law to grapple with its own traumatic past.

The text of *Colonel Chabert* is in effect the story of a young lawyer's attempt to recognize and to respond to this peculiar claim to restitution of property. Chabert tells the lawyer how he died in war without quite dying: how he was wounded and buried alive in battle; how he was mistakenly declared dead; and how he managed to struggle out of the mass grave, only to find a society that denies his existence and a wife, now remarried and with children, who refuses to acknowledge his letters. Astonished by the appearance of Chabert but willing to believe his story, the lawyer Derville suggests a compromise between Chabert and his wife, a settlement that will provide an equitable compromise on the property. In the story of the compromise and of its failure—through which the text stages the drama of the legal struggle to come alive before the law—Balzac describes the very struggle of the survivor of catastrophe to reclaim life: to claim existence and identity. But it is also, I will argue, through the peculiar legal struggle over the claim to property that Balzac shows how the law, in this tale, at the same time comes to recognize, and fails fully to comprehend, the legacy of a traumatic history.

HAUNTED PROPERTY

I

The problem of recognition is indeed central to the opening scene of the text. In the very first lines of the story, a clerk at a lawyer's office notes the strange appearance of a figure that keeps returning to their door:

"Look! There's that old greatcoat again!" . . .

"Simonnin, stop playing stupid tricks on people. . . . No matter how poor a client is, he's still a man, damn it!" said the head clerk. . . .

"If he's a *man*, why'd you call him *old greatcoat*?" asked Simonnin.[1]

Appearing only as a ghostly "greatcoat," the stranger's first encounter with the law is marked by a misrecognition, an inability of the law office to decide whether the figure should be considered fully human. Haunting the office in his not fully recognizable form, this figure of a *man without property* situates the question of property at the very heart and at the jurisprudential center of the law.

The scene that the stranger interrupts in fact represents the performance of the law at a very specific historical moment, a moment that is named by the clerk who is improvising a long and "prolix" appeal:

> *But in his noble and benevolent wisdom, His Majesty, Louis the Eighteenth . . . [deemed to] repair the damages caused by the terrible and sorry disasters of our revolutionary times by restoring to his loyal and numerous adherents . . . all their unsold property . . . rendered on . . . June 1814. (2–4)*[2]

The lawyer's appeal refers, specifically, to the period of the Restoration, the time of the return of the Bourbon monarchy to the throne after the abdication of Napoleon and, more precisely, to the Charter of 1814 by which the new king, Louis XVIII, took power. In its political significance, this moment was an attempt at a kind of historical return: France's attempt to return to a form of rule that existed before the Revolution and to create a bridge over the rupture constituted by the radical events of 1789 and their consequences during the Napoleonic Empire. But this moment was in fact, as the lawyer's appeal indicates, a legal one as well; for the Charter of 1814 was the reiteration and modification, in particular, of the legal legacy of the Revolution: of the astounding legal breakthrough of the *Declaration of the Rights of Man and Citizen of 1789* and its codification during the Napoleonic Empire in the Civil Code. The Restoration's legal and political attempt to return to the past, Balzac suggests, thus takes place through the execution and the institution of another kind of return: the return of property to the aristocrats from whom it had been taken during the Revolution. The return of property in the legal act of the Restoration is thus a political attempt to return to the pre-Revolutionary past.

The primary interest in Balzac's text is not, however, in this story of restoration per se but in the way in which it becomes bound up with a far stranger kind of return: the peculiar manner in which the return of property becomes entangled, strangely, with the insistent and uncanny return of the dead. The appearance of the stranger at the door of the office indeed represents not simply a man who is poor but, more enigmatically, a man who cannot be recognized, precisely, as alive:

> "Monsieur," Boucard said to him, "would you be good enough to give us your name, so that our Master may know . . . "
> "Chabert."
> "Isn't that the colonel who died at Eylau?" . . .
> "The same, Monsieur," answered the good man with old-fashioned simplicity. (10–11)

It is indeed as a man who is dead that Chabert first introduces himself into the scene of the law: "My death," he will later reassert to his lawyer, "is a matter of historical record." Coming nonetheless to make a claim for his property, he appears as a peculiar inversion of the historical attempt to return to the past effected by the Restoration. At the point that the Restoration would return property to the aristocrats, here a figure of the Revolution comes to demand that his own property be returned to him. In the very act of making this claim in the name of a dead man, however, Chabert also points toward a past that cannot be spoken in the simple terms of the living. If property here functions, from within the Restoration, as the place par excellence of return, it is also, in this story, the uncanny site of a haunting.

If we step back for a moment, we can see how Balzac's narrative about a dead man coming before the law addresses a larger question of law and historical memory, specifically as they became intertwined after the French Revolution. For the introduction of the Charter of 1814 in the opening scene of Balzac's story inscribes this legal document in the literary text not only in relation to the Charter's use of law to return aristocratic property but also and more profoundly, I would suggest, in the Charter's peculiar function as a decree of historical forgetting. Indeed, quite remarkably, when Louis XVIII proclaimed his kingship after the abdication of Napoleon, he placed in the Charter an article that, in François Furet's words, "put forgetfulness under the law's protection, as if it were the most precious of national virtues: 'All research into opinions and votes issued up to the Restoration is prohibited. Courts and citizens are equally commanded to forget.'"[3] Decreeing forgetting within the very Charter that reiterates the Civil Code as the regime's basic legal principles, the king makes of forgetting itself a legal function. Appearing against the background of this operation of the Charter, Chabert's return before the law can thus be understood as the return of memory against the legal attempt to forget. The claim to property, in other words, is the site of a memory: the memory of a revolutionary history paradoxically repressed within the very extension of the Revolution's own legal legacy.[4]

But such a claim is not made in the light of day. It is significant that Chabert's story and his claim literally emerge not in the outer offices of the clerks who work during the day but in the inner office of the "master" lawyer, Derville, who works, we are told, "only at night." Not available to the law's consciousness, the story of Chabert is narrated to the lawyer in the darkness of the night, as the return of an ungrasped death that insists on legal recognition. Indeed, Derville's nighttime labor seems to represent a place of unconscious wakefulness at the very heart of the law. The claim to property profoundly and symbolically becomes, thus, the unconscious site on which the law confronts the nightmare of a historical trauma.

2

The story that Chabert comes to tell is in fact tied up with a crucial moment in the record of French history: Chabert is a colonel in Napoleon's army who was involved in the famous battle of Eylau and who was instrumental in Murat's charge—an actual military event that has been called the "greatest charge of the Napoleonic wars."[5] To the extent that his name is recognizable, then, Chabert represents the greatness of the Napoleonic period, the spreading of the principles of the Revolution throughout Europe, and the greatness of military glory so central to French identity. Indeed, it is in preparing the way for Murat's charge, apparently, that Chabert is wounded, falls off his horse, and is subsequently trampled under the charging soldiers. His recognizable historical identity, he suggests, is based purely on the mistakes of medics and more importantly on a mistaken legal declaration:

> Those damned medics, who had just seen me trampled beneath the horses' hooves of two regiments, no doubt dispensed with checking my pulse and declared that I was quite dead. My death certificate was then probably made out in accordance with the rules of military jurisprudence. (20)

Although he is truly a Napoleonic colonel, Chabert's official historical status as a hero of the wars—and in particular of its "victories and conquests"—is associated with the finality and tragic romance of his death, a death that is, as it turns out, a legal fiction. In this error of death, then, the law of certificates and declarations has paradoxically helped to write a heroic history that eliminates the reality of war—a reality of horror, of atrocity, and of confusion in which death is carried on into life and which Chabert, in contrast, is precisely struggling to articulate and to narrate.

The reality of which Chabert speaks is indeed a far more gruesome one than the romantic story of his death, associated with the greatness of French victory. The death in this tale is of an entirely different order:

> When I woke up, Monsieur, I was in a position and a setting which I couldn't convey to you if I talked till dawn. The little air I was breathing was foul. I wanted to move but had no room. Opening my eyes, I saw nothing. . . . I heard, or thought I heard—though I can't swear to it—groans coming from the pile of corpses I was lying in. Even though the memory of these moments is murky, and despite the fact I must have endured even greater suffering, there are nights when I still think I hear those muffled moans! But there was something more awful: a silence that I have never experienced anywhere else, the perfect silence of the grave. (21–22)

What Chabert truly comes to know is not the glorious death of war and conquest but the horror of being buried alive under the dead. The story he has to tell is indeed the story of the dead, the sounds of the dead in the very act of dying, and the "silence of the grave" itself, a silence far more horrible, he suggests, than the loud and noisy heroism of the death named on the historian's page. Likewise, the triumph he also achieves in this horrible situation—the victory over death he will accomplish—is not the victory of war as recorded in history but an underground story horrible in its gruesome detail:

> Scrabbling around me at once, for there was no time to lose, I felt a huge, detached arm. I owe my rescue to that bone. Without it I would have perished! But with a fury I'm sure you can imagine, I plowed my way through the corpses separating me from the surface. A layer of earth had no doubt been thrown over us—I say 'us' as if the others were still alive! I still do not know how I could have dug through all that flesh. It formed a barrier between me and life. But I went at it, Monsieur, and here I am. (22–23)

Chabert's story of his return to life is not a glorious tale of conquest but the horrid account of tearing human limbs and of climbing on human bodies in a desperate attempt to save himself and to struggle out of the grave. Indeed, his final emergence from the grave conveys a certain disrespect, a paradoxical act of desecration of the dead rather than their simple veneration and glorification: "'I pushed myself up with my feet standing on the solid backs of dead men. This was no time to respect the dead'" (23).

In words uncomfortably anticipatory of twentieth-century horrors—one thinks, for example, of the stories of people in the gas chambers stepping on each other in an attempt to resist choking and get air—Chabert describes a struggle for survival that cannot be assimilated to heroic notions of greatness or of triumph.[6] Not being really dead, Chabert in fact serves as a witness to a death—and a survival—far more disturbing and far less comprehensible than the deaths and victories recorded in official history. What comes back thus, through the "realism" of Balzac's description of Chabert's experience in the mass grave is in this sense truly a traumatic return: a history of death that insists on returning precisely to the extent that it is not fully understood.

What the literary text suggests surprisingly, however, is that, if history is to be understood as a traumatic history, its insistent return should not be located simply in the psychic suffering of Chabert but, oddly and problematically, within the inscription of this suffering in the realm of the law. Chabert himself suggests, repeatedly, that it is not his physical suffering that is of interest. Indeed, just as the lawyer Derville gets caught up in the physical and actual horrors of Chabert's story, Chabert insists that its import lies somewhere else:

> "Monsieur," said the attorney, "you are confusing me. I feel like I've been dreaming. Just hold on a moment."
>
> "You are the only person," said the Colonel with a sorrowful look, "who has had the patience to listen to me. I haven't found a lawyer willing to advance me ten napoleons to send to Germany for the necessary documents to begin my lawsuit . . . "
>
> "What lawsuit?" said the attorney, who had forgotten his client's present painful position while listening to his past sufferings.
>
> "Monsieur, the Countess Ferraud is my wife! She possesses 30,000 pounds a year that belong to me, and she won't give me a sou. When I tell these things to lawyers, to men of good sense; when I propose that I, a beggar, should sue a count and countess; when I, a dead man, rise up against a death certificate, marriage licenses, and birth certificates, they show me the door. . . . I've been buried beneath the dead, but now I'm buried beneath the living; beneath certificates, facts—the whole society would rather have me buried underground!" (26–27)

If Derville is first moved by the story of Chabert's physical and mental sufferings—his remarkable story of being buried alive—what Chabert is troubled by is another form of burial, the burial beneath the living. If the war trauma can be said to repeat itself, indeed, it repeats itself not in Chabert's physical or mental suffering but in his suffering before the law: in his inability, having revived himself physically, to revive himself legally. The trauma returns, that is, not in a vision of his remembered near-suffocation in the grave but in his present and repeated suffocation by the death certificates and by the legal papers that bury him alive in a more pernicious and more permanent way. The repetition of the trauma, therefore, takes the form, not of a physical or mental, but of a social and a legal, death.[7] As such, the horror of the traumatic history is contained, in this story, in the enigmatic and complex problem of a legal trauma.

3

Chabert's ghostly reappearance before Derville, indeed, is represented not as an anomaly coming to the law from outside it but as a problem that haunts it, as it were, from within. The dead colonel's mistaken burial had first occurred in a battle that was part of an attempt to spread the central principles of the Revolution in the form of the Civil Code—the law that, in 1807 (the very year of the battle of Eylau), was named after Napoleon and was considered by him to be one of his greatest achievements.[8] Chabert returns from this battle, however, not as a conqueror spreading the law in its glory but as the war's victim, as the man mutilated and barely recognizable as human precisely because of a war meant to disseminate the notion of rights. If revolutionary law in a certain sense redefined the human around the notion of rights, Chabert emerges from among the literally dehumanized, the disarticulated limbs and unrecognizable faces of those upon whom and through whom these rights were imposed. Chabert's return thus haunts the law with an aspect of its own history that remains unrecognizable to it, a figure of inhumanity that the law cannot contain within its own memory.

Chabert does not return, indeed, precisely as a human being claiming his rights but as a cry for humanity emanating from someone not yet recognized as human. Chabert must claim, first, his very existence, his very recognizability as a living human being who has the right to claim. Describing to Derville his attempts to contact his wife, Chabert displays the depth of his dilemma caused by this radical refusal of recognition:

"Well," said the Colonel, with a gesture of concentrated rage, "when I called under an assumed name I was not received, and the day I used my own I was pushed out the door. . . . My gaze would plunge inside that carriage, which passed by with lightning speed, and barely catch a glimpse of the woman who is my wife and yet no longer mine. Oh, since that day I have lived for vengeance!" (33)

The desire for rebirth before the law, as Chabert first speaks of it, emerges as a cry of revenge that would force recognition through an act of retribution: an act of forcefully reclaiming the life that he no longer owns. In claiming his property, then, Chabert does not claim something to which he has the right but rather that to which he precisely can no longer rightfully lay claim, a self, a love, and a life of which he has been radically dispossessed.

A PLACE OF MEMORY

4

From one perspective, the entire narrative of Balzac's novel—the legal drama that grows out of the encounter between Chabert and Derville—can be understood as revealing the law's capacity to hear this claim and to perform the rebirth of the dead man, his legal resuscitation, through its capability of translating the traumatic story into recognizable legal terms. Derville could be said to discover in the claim more than the negotiation of an already existing link between the legally unrecognizable figure and the human world he wishes to enter. The claim to self and to life, made as a claim to property—as a claim that is always made in relation to another—becomes, in Derville's creative manipulation of it, the possibility for Chabert to achieve a recognizable identity.

Indeed, if Derville is shown to be a capable listener, this legal listening is made possible, in part, not because he speaks in the same language as Chabert, but because he integrates the story—and the claim—into a recognizable legal and human framework. As it turns out, Derville is also the lawyer for Chabert's (now remarried) wife, and it is by bringing Chabert into relation to her, by proposing a form of mutual legal recognition, that Derville first responds to Chabert's cry:

> "This is a serious matter," [Derville] said at last, somewhat mechanically. . . . "I need to think about this case with a clear head; it is quite unusual."
>
> "Well," the Colonel answered coldly, raising his head proudly, "if I lose, I may die, but not alone." Suddenly the old man disappeared, and the eyes of a young soldier ignited with the fires of desire and vengeance.
>
> "We might have to compromise," said the lawyer.
>
> "Compromise?" repeated Colonel Chabert. "Am I dead or am I alive?"
>
> "Monsieur," continued the lawyer, "I hope you will follow my advice. Your cause is mine." (34)

While Chabert's claim is a cry for retribution, Derville's response translates this symmetry of destruction into the reciprocal recognition of a settlement.[9]

He recognizes in the cry, that is, the claim for rights, which thus permits him to accord the unrecognizable figure before him the recognition of a human being. Explaining calmly to Chabert that his wife is remarried, has children, and has manipulated the inheritance in a way that makes it untraceable to Chabert, the lawyer offers a solution that will not return Chabert to the past he once lived but will allow some recompense for its loss.

Indeed, as the lawyer makes clear, the need for a negotiation of a legal solution imposes itself precisely because Chabert's claim to survival comes into direct confrontation with that of his wife. Upon hearing the news of her husband's death on the battlefield, Mme. Chabert had, we are told, remarried an aristocratic count, the Count Ferraud, whose name she proceeded to take as her own and with whom she had two children. Working with her pension from Chabert's death and with her inheritance, she had made use of the monetary swings of the early Restoration to manipulate this sum into a small fortune, thus providing a place for herself in Restoration society as a wealthy and aristocratic countess. But her husband, the count, now has ambitions of his own and, she senses, has been looking for an excuse to divorce her so as to marry into the royal family and have a chance at becoming a peer of France, an excuse that Chabert's return and her unwitting bigamy would provide. If Chabert feels he cannot quite come alive, then, if he suffers a social death through what constitutes his wife's survival, Mme. Ferraud is horrified that he cannot quite die, that his survival means likewise a social death for her. The lawyer's offer of compromise thus mediates between two opposing claims to survival.

The conflict and the compromise, moreover, take place as a negotiation about, and through, property; it is through property (his name, marriage, and money) that Chabert makes a claim for his identity, and it is through property (her wealth and marriage) that the wife resists. But it is also because this property is ultimately negotiable that the claim can become a settlement and be recognized on both sides.[10] Derville thus suggests that Chabert give up his claim to the marriage (by annulling the marriage contract) if Mme. Ferraud agrees to grant Chabert his identity (by annulling the death certificate). Derville convinces Chabert to negotiate, in addition, because he cannot afford a lawsuit and will ultimately lose his name, while Derville convinces the wife to negotiate so that she can avoid the consequences of a lawsuit that would expose her bigamy to her husband. Chabert's identity as a living Colonel Chabert (through the annulment of the death certificate) and the wife's identity as Mme. Ferraud (through the annulment of the previous marriage contract to Chabert) are thus established and brought into relation to each other as reciprocal acts of annulment that treat the establishment of identity as a kind of exchange of properties. The right to property, by establishing an analogy between the asymmetrical needs and claims of Chabert and his wife—between the man who has as yet no property and the woman who is at risk of losing hers—thus becomes the mediating term by which the law brings the two parties together and whose principle governs the very form of the compromise. In this sense the claim to property—in its powers not only to recognize but, more fundamentally, to constitute a recognizable symmetry of identities—becomes the epitome of the right to claim that is also the necessity of the mutual recognition of one another's rights.[11]

5

The legal remedy of compromise is also represented, in the story, as an act of remembering. In effecting Chabert's legal rebirth through the compromise—by associating and recognizing his life with a legal form—Derville could be said to reenact Chabert's rebirth from the pit as the memory of an earlier, legal birth, the birth of man as a subject of rights in the legal act of foundation constituted by the Revolution. The law, in resuscitating Chabert, thus remembers through him the legal foundation of the subject created by the *Declaration*, as a "juridical person" recognizable through his right to claim and, specifically, the right to claim his property. Against the background of the reduced notion of property as mere possession, Derville thus resuscitates, with Chabert, the sense in which the *Declaration of the Rights of Man and Citizen*, rather than recognizing the human through his property, precisely constituted the subject as proprietor, as the one who is recognized through his very right to claim.[12]

This act of resurrecting the original legal meaning of the revolutionary subject is thus also represented in Balzac's text as the possibility of recreating a smooth succession between past and present and incorporating the legal history of the Revolution and post-Revolutionary periods (the extended history of the Revolution as the foundation of modern law) into the continuity of a nontraumatic history. Moving between Chabert (who is trying to live like a Napoleonic colonel) and his wife (who is trying to live the life of a Restoration countess), Derville ultimately convinces both of them to come to his office to negotiate the settlement, which he stages in a highly theatrical gesture by directing Chabert, dressed in the uniform of the Imperial Guard, and his wife, dressed in her most glorious Restoration garb, to sit in separate rooms while he moves between them, reading the settlement.[13] In this scene, Derville symbolically crosses the gap between Empire and Restoration—the end of the Napoleonic Empire represented by the moment of Chabert's so-called death—and turns it into the legal memory of the Revolution, not as the "endless abyss" that cannot be bridged, but as a beginning with an end, a moment in the past that gives meaning and sense to the history that it created. He also, in this sense, restores Napoleon in history, not as the conqueror who spread the Code through catastrophic wars, but as the ruler responsible for creating a place of memory in the Code.[14] The legal settlement of property, the remedy to historical trauma proposed by Derville, thus situates the legal Code as a place of memory, the memory of the Revolution as the beginning of a continuous and comprehensible history and the recognition of the human as, precisely, the reflection and embodiment of the Code.

THE ENACTMENT OF WITNESS

6

Yet if, on the one hand, Derville's listening acts as a kind of legal memory of the history of the law, it also comes to enact something within that history that it still fails to comprehend.

This incomprehension occurs, moreover, around the very problem of property. Although Derville seems able to appreciate what it means for Chabert not to have property, he appears to misunderstand what it means for his wife to cling so desperately to it. Indeed, while Chabert tells Derville directly what he refers to as "'the secret of my situation'" (19), that is, of his burial and return from underneath the corpses, the wife does not fully reveal to Derville what the narrator calls the "secrets of her conduct deep in her heart" (59), another burial and another story that is not possessed by the wife any more than Chabert's story is possessed by him. Mme. Ferraud's exchange of husbands and manipulation of her inheritance from Chabert is in fact an attempt, we are told, to hide her own past life in a brothel, the place from which Chabert had originally taken her and which she is still trying to forget in her marriage to Count Ferraud and in her attempt to become a "proper lady." But Count Ferraud is himself trying to escape another past: the history of his own father, who lost his property during the Terror, a loss of status that Count Ferraud is desperately attempting to repair in his ambitions to become a peer of France. In the negotiation of the settlement, then, the problem of property, even while it brings Chabert and Mme. Ferraud in relation to each other, also represents an abyss of history that cannot be fully grasped by the legal Code.[15] For them, it is clear, the law represents not what brings them into history but what continues to keep them out of it. Their relation to one another is determined, thus, not through their established identities and histories but through what, in each history, neither can fully possess.

Indeed, Mme. Ferraud is no more a Restoration countess than Chabert can be said to be, properly speaking, a colonel of the Empire. Her desperate attempts to hide her past indicate, in fact, the ways in which she has not quite managed to achieve the period role that she wishes to portray. And this is linked, moreover, to the way in which the law has harmed not only Chabert but her as well; for the Civil Code in fact restricted the rights of women over spousal property in the rules of inheritance.[16] What Chabert and Mme. Ferraud truly share, as it turns out, is the way in which neither is quite situated within the period he or she wishes to represent; Chabert is too late to be, any longer, a colonel of the Empire, and Mme. Ferraud has not yet achieved the full status of a countess of the Restoration.[17] In this sense, their communication with each other, in the negotiation, takes place across their secrets, from one abyss to another, a story that is carried on beneath the negotiation Derville is so valiantly attempting to maneuver.[18]

Property is, in other words, not only the rational principle by which the negotiation becomes possible but also, in this story, the one thing that escapes all rational principles and hence causes the compromise ultimately to fail.

7

Indeed, the story of the settlement—which is the story of the capacity of the law to recognize and to remember history as the history of the legal subject—ultimately turns into the story of its failure: of the reenactment of another aspect of the law's own history that the language and memory of the Code does not fully comprehend. It is, moreover, precisely around the monetary terms of the property settlement that the failure of the compromise takes place. Sitting in separate rooms as Derville walks between them and reads the paper, Chabert and his wife listen quietly until the matter of the property settlement is broached:

"But that is much too much!" said the Countess. . . .
"What do you want, Madame?"
"I want . . . "
" . . . him to remain dead," Derville broke in quickly. . . .
"Monsieur," said the Countess, "if it is a matter of 24,000 francs a year, then we will go to court . . . "
"Yes, we will go to court," cried the muffled voice of the Colonel, who opened the door and suddenly appeared before his wife, one hand in his

waistcoat and the other hanging by his side, a gesture given terrible significance by the memory of his adventure.

"It's him," said the countess to herself.

"Too much?" repeated the old soldier. "I gave you nearly a million and
you are haggling over my misery. . . . We hold our property in common, our
marriage is not dissolved . . . "

"But Monsieur is not Colonel Chabert!" cried the Countess, feigning
surprise. (73–74)

Refusing the terms of the property settlement, the countess is suddenly confronted by the figure of Chabert in person, a direct confrontation that, rather
than producing the recognition arranged by the legal papers, produces precisely the refusal of recognition that the settlement was supposed to correct.
This encounter and this refusal of recognition break the theatrical staging
of memory that should bring Chabert to life and reenact, once more, his
death: a death that, it appears, could never quite be grasped within the Code's
legal forms.

This return of death in the wife's refusal also brings back the return of
Chabert's cry for vengeance:

"Well, Colonel," [said Derville,] "I was right, wasn't I, to urge you not
to come in? . . . You have lost our suit; your wife knows that you are unrecognizable."

"I will shoot her!"

"Madness! You will be caught and executed." (74–75)

Rather than remembering (and correcting) the past of Chabert's life, the law
becomes the very site of the reenactment of his death, of the original blow
that began the incomprehensible story of Chabert's death on the battlefield:
"The poor Colonel . . . walked slowly down the steps of the dark staircase,
lost in somber thoughts, perhaps overcome by the blow he had just suffered—
so cruelly and deeply did it penetrate his heart" (75). In the reenactment of
the death, the law becomes the scene not simply of the memory of its own
revolutionary past but of a secret buried at the heart of this history, the in-
extricability of law and history that constitutes the foundation of the human
as the legal subject and that enigmatically also constitutes history, precisely,
as the history of a trauma.

It is, therefore, not only in the capacity of the law to remember but in
the failure of memory within the law, Balzac suggests, that another truth of
the revolutionary past begins to emerge. The nonfulfillment of the compromise does not simply represent a failure of the law to understand or witness

history; rather, it shows history as emerging (and being borne witness to) precisely through the law's own failures. The scene of failed settlement thus reproduces the figure of the survivor at the moment of the intended compromise and recognition (the figure of the "'nonproprietor,' 'devoid of property,' or dispossessed" that, in Etienne Balibar's words, would be, precisely, a "contradiction in terms" within the framework of Revolutionary law).[19] If the Code remembers the truth of revolutionary history as the right to claim—as a right recognizable through the claim to property—the Code also inscribes *within it* the haunting figure of the survivor attending upon this very act, not as the one who speaks his rights but as the unspeakable, the mute survivor, attending upon and yet not recognized within the framework of revolutionary law.[20] Between the possibility of compromise and its failure, then, the law serves, here, as a double site of witness: the witness of the human as a claim and the witness of the one who cannot be recognized as human. The law is at the same time a witness to the human grounded in the legal act of speech and a witness to the survivor appearing only as a muteness at the heart of the law.

The scene of failure thus also marks a peculiar doubling at the center of revolutionary history: an entanglement of two histories founded precisely in the impossibility of their analogy and their negotiation. The failure of the compromise represents not only the denial of Chabert's identity but also the denial of the divorce, a legal collapse that, paradoxically, binds the two parties around a gap, and resituates revolutionary history in the splitting and binding of these two incommensurable pasts.

ANOTHER FREEDOM

8

It might appear that this failure establishes a relation between law and history in a kind of death drive that condemns the law to participate in the repetitions of an incomprehensible catastrophe.[21] Many critics have read the end of the story simply as a confirmation of the failure of Chabert to attain his identity in a corrupt Restoration society.[22] In the last section of the tale, Chabert, after leaving Derville's office, is seduced by his wife to go to her country estate, where she produces another theatrical setting, a setting in which she appears with her children before Chabert and convinces him that her own survival and the unity of her family depend upon his willingness to sign another legal paper in which he would give up his name and profess himself a fraud in exchange for a small pension. In an act of love, Chabert is about to agree to sign when he accidentally overhears his wife suggesting that he be locked up in a madhouse. At this moment Chabert steps before his wife, refuses to sign the paper, and promises never to reclaim his name, ultimately going off to live as a vagabond and, in the final scenes of the novel, in an almshouse.

This hardly makes for a happy ending. But it is in this last part of the story, in the lingering afterlife of the relationship between Chabert and his wife and in Chabert's persistent survivals of his repeated experiences of failure and death that, I would propose, the true potential of the compromise, as a beginning of a different form of historical witness, comes to be articulated. It is in Chabert's refusal of his wife's offer, I would argue—and in the manner it repeats and reclaims the catastrophe of the first scene of refusal—that the story opens the possibility for Chabert to name himself anew, through the very failure to achieve his former identity.[23] This new act creates a possibility that is born from, but not contained by, the law's previous attempt and failure to turn the past into an identity and a possession.

This possibility will appear in the moment of the second scene of signing, in which Chabert refuses to sign his wife's paper written up by the corrupt lawyer Delbecq. The scene is, in fact, a repetition of the scene of failure in Derville's office but in a form that reverses its effects. In this second scene, Chabert truly gives up vengeance for the first time and does so, moreover, as the making of a promise:

> "Madame," he said after staring at her a moment and forcing her to blush, "Madame, I do not curse you; I despise you. I thank fate for severing our ties. I do not even feel a desire for vengeance, I no longer love you. I want nothing from you. Live peacefully on the honor of my word; it is worth more than the scribblings of all the notaries in Paris. I will never lay claim to the name I may have made illustrious. I am nothing but a poor devil named Hyacinthe, who asks only for a good spot to sit in the sun. Farewell." (89–90)

The act of refusal to sign the paper, here, is an act of renunciation. The giving up of vengeance, through the refusal to sign the legal agreement, precisely repeats the legal failure of the previous scene, but does so not in the form of passive repetition but rather as a new kind of action: as a promise not to reclaim the name that was refused him in the first scene of signing. The self that emerges, here, is not the self of the past, the "Chabert" that is no longer fully possible, but rather "Hyacinthe," Chabert's given name, which emerges in the promise never to reclaim—that is, to refrain from repeatedly and compulsively returning to claim—the name Chabert.[24] This is not a triumphant reassertion of identity but, instead, the peculiar capacity to name, precisely, his very survival in the form of an ultimate loss: "Not Chabert! Not Chabert!" he says when he is addressed by his old name, "My name is Hyacinthe. . . . I am no longer a man, I am number 164, room 7" (98).

We could say, then, that in the act of renunciation and promise, Chabert reclaims the failure of the law as the very condition of his freedom.[25] In giving up the claim, Chabert could perhaps be said, in Emmanuel Levinas's words, to retain a different kind of claim, the "claim to judge history—that is to say, to remain free with regard to events, whatever the internal logic binding them."[26] Chabert will retain, in the final scenes, an ongoing link to his military past—he continues to speak of Napoleon and addresses some passing Prussians with disdain—but he no longer appears to consider this past as a matter of his own possession. It constitutes, rather, a memory and a relation to history that, if they are Chabert's only remaining property, are no longer a property that could simply be possessed.

9

It is in this peculiar way in which Chabert lives on beyond his own name that his survival—and the traumatic history to which he bears witness—first becomes truly legible. No longer "a man," as he says—that is, a subject defined entirely in the law's own terms—Chabert is nonetheless still recognizable as he appears again before the eyes of the lawyer. Precisely because he has failed; because he has survived beyond the name Chabert, can this figure and his history emerge to be read and witnessed in another way. In this act, indeed, Chabert is once again seen by the law, no longer recognized through the compromise but encountered in a scene of witnessing that also appears as Derville's own form of giving up.[27]

In the final lines of the story, thus, Derville, with the young lawyer Godeschal whom he has mentored, happen to pass Chabert as they are on the way to a town outside Paris. Chabert, covered in poor clothing and sitting outside an almshouse, is not recognizable to Godeschal but is immediately recognized by Derville. Standing in front of the man who now names himself by a number, Derville remarks on the fate of Chabert and ends with an impassioned speech to the young lawyer who was once his student:

> "I have learned so much practicing my profession! . . . I have seen wills
> burned. I have seen mothers rob their children. . . . I cannot tell you every-
> thing I have seen because I have seen crimes that justice is powerless to
> rectify. In the end, none of the horrors that novelists believe they've invented
> can compare to the truth. You'll soon become acquainted with such charm-

ing things yourself; as for me, I am moving to the country with my wife. I am sick of Paris."

"I have seen plenty already," Godeschal replied. (100–101)

This scene, I would propose, is an ultimate scene of legal witnessing, not as the memory Derville had hoped to accomplish with the compromise, but as the seeing of something he cannot completely tell: "I cannot tell you everything I have seen," he says, "because I have seen crimes that justice is powerless to rectify." In this scene, then, the lawyer appears, peculiarly, as witness to what cannot be told simply in legal terms. Seeing Chabert before him, the lawyer Derville comes to recognize, and to articulate, the law's own limits. In the face of his own failure, he speaks in a language that, like the novelist he invokes, can only approach but never fully capture the sight of the figure before him. The law bears witness, in this way, to what remains outside it. As such, this witness is not so much offered as a reflection on the past but as a scene of teaching, as the words passed on to a student, and to a reader, who will learn from them only in the future.[28]

PART TWO

After the End

CHAPTER THREE

Lying and History

Hannah Arendt, "Truth and Politics" and "Lying in Politics"

I WOULD LIKE TO ADDRESS the problem of violence in the political realm by focusing on a question that emerges out of several late works by the twentieth-century political thinker Hannah Arendt: What is history in the time of what Arendt calls "the modern lie"? In "Truth and Politics" (1967) and "Lying in Politics" (1971), Arendt reflects on what she considers a profound philosophical conundrum at the heart of politics and the political: an intimate and foundational relation between politics and the lie that has momentous implications for the way we think about political history (and, more widely, about history as such). Beginning from a reflection on the nature of political action in the context of lying, Arendt ultimately enables a rethinking of the very nature of history around the possibility of its political denial. What does it mean, she asks, for political history to be fundamentally linked, at certain points in modern times, to its erasure or lack of witness? And how might it be possible to witness from within this history?

POLITICS AND THE LIE

The question of history arises, in "Truth and Politics," in the context of Arendt's concern with the pervasive role of lying within the political sphere in the modern world. As Arendt had suggested in her earlier work, *The Human Condition*, the sphere of politics is important because it is the exemplary place in which man displays his essential capacity, as man, to act and thus to bring into the world "something new ... which cannot be expected from whatever may have happened before."[1] This concept of political action arose specifically in the Greek polis, she says, when words and deeds replaced the mute force of violence and created a public sphere in which men appeared before each other and created the world anew in unpredictable and unexpected ways. But the political sphere maintains itself, Arendt adds, not only as the site of action but also as the site of its remembrance, for "speech and action . . . possess an enduring quality of their own because they create their own remembrance."[2] More specifically, they create political bodies that establish the conditions for remembrance, "that is, for history."[3] History thus seems central to the functioning of the political world, both as its memory and as the ground upon which the political world builds a future.

In the modern world, however, Arendt will point out in "Truth and Politics," the public realm has become a realm of deception, a place dramatizing, in effect, the "clash of factual truth and politics, which we witness today on such a large scale."[4] Arendt draws on a number of examples, remarking, for instance, on the disappearance of Trotsky from the history books of the Soviet Union, and on the German and French representations of their actions during World War II. Unlike the ancient world, in which the notion of politics first appeared, she suggests, the public realm in the modern world is not only the place of political action that creates history but also, and centrally, the place of the political lie that denies it. Focusing on the ubiquity of the lie in the modern world, then, Arendt ultimately asks the following question: What kind of politics is possible in a world in which history is regularly and systematically denied?

The topic of the denial of history emerges, for Arendt, after the great wars. The phenomenon had been analyzed in the work of another great writer, Sigmund Freud, in terms of the psychological forms of denial in the face of catastrophic events, and especially those of World War I.[5] But Arendt's explicit concern in her essay is of another nature, a form of deliberate political deception that also emerges after that war but, in a surprisingly brazen way, arises directly and consciously in the political sphere and attacks the fundamental facts of history that had previously been considered indestructible:

During the twenties, so a story goes, Clemenceau, shortly before his death, found himself engaged in a friendly talk with a representative of the Weimar Republic on the question of guilt for the outbreak of the First World War. "What, in your opinion," Clemenceau was asked, "will future historians think of this troublesome and controversial issue?" He replied, "This I don't know. But I know for certain that they will not say Belgium invaded Germany." We are concerned here with brutally elementary data of this kind, whose indestructibility has been taken for granted even by the most extreme and most sophisticated believers in historicism. (TP, 239)[6]

The responsibility for the outbreak of World War I—a matter of profound political significance between the wars—is a factual truth that, in an earlier period, might have seemed unassailable even in the contested world of politics. But in the political world that emerged in the ensuing period, even this crucial and well-known fact had come under debate:

> It is true, considerably more than the whims of historians would be needed to eliminate from the record the fact that on the night of August 4, 1914, German troops crossed the frontier of Belgium; it would require no less than a power monopoly over the entire civilized world. But such a power monopoly is far from being inconceivable, and it is not difficult to imagine what the fate of factual truth would be if power interests, national or social, had the last say in these matters. (TP, 239)

In her allusion to the totalitarian states that arose after World War I, Arendt suggests that the world in which facts could be agreed upon is in danger of changing forever and that not only individual facts but the fate of "factual truth" as such is in danger in this new and emergent reality. The danger to the political world in modern times is the loss of the factual world that emerges, paradoxically, at the heart of the political realm, which ordinarily creates, and depends upon, historical remembrance.

What is of interest to Arendt is that the lie comes not from without, but precisely from within, the realm of political action and is in fact tied to it by a fundamental similarity between action and lying. Facts are fragile in the political sphere, she says, because truth-telling is actually much less political in its nature than the lie:

> The hallmark of factual truth is that its opposite is neither error nor illusion . . . but the deliberate falsehood or lie. Error of course is possible. . . . But the point is that with respect to facts there exists another alternative, and this alternative, the deliberate falsehood, does not belong to the same species as propositions that, whether right or mistaken, intend no more than to say what is or how something that is appears to me. A factual statement—Germany invaded Belgium in August 1914—acquires political implications only by being put in an interpretative context. But the opposite proposition, which Clemenceau, still unacquainted with the art of rewriting history, thought absurd, needs no context to be of political significance. It is clearly an attempt to change the record, and as such it is a form of *action*. (TP, 249)

If the lie "changes the record" of history, it does so, Arendt suggests, not as a falsehood that negates a truth (a falsehood that could be a mere error without being a lie) but as an act of speech intended, like political action, to make a change in the world. The liar thus prevails in the political world because, like the actor, he is exercising freedom:

> While the liar is a man of action, the truth teller . . . most emphatically is not. . . . The liar . . . needs no . . . accommodation to appear on the political scene; he has the great advantage that he always is, so to speak, already in the midst of it. He is an actor by nature; he says what is not so because he wants things to be different from what they are—that is, he wants to change the world. He takes advantage of the undeniable affinity of our capacity for action, for changing reality, with this mysterious faculty of ours that enables us to *say*, "The sun is shining," when it is raining cats and dogs. . . . In other words, our ability to lie—but not necessarily our ability to tell the truth—belongs among the few obvious, demonstrable data that confirm human freedom. That we can change the circumstances under which we live at all is because we are relatively free from them, and it is this freedom that is abused and perverted through mendacity. (TP, 250–51)

Like the political actor, the political liar wishes to change the world, to be free from things as they are given. Since his denial of the world is also a form of action, the act of lying is, in itself, a demonstration of freedom. The lie does not appear in the political realm only as the denial of the historical acts of the past, then, but also as a kind of *action of beginning* that, potentially, has its own political and historical unfolding.[7]

It is this independent historical unfolding that, in fact, Arendt describes as the site of the danger of the lie when she narrates the passage of the lie from its traditional role, within politics, as another means of effecting true political action, to a wholly independent and all-consuming activity that replaces action (and its history) altogether. Thus at first, Arendt argues, lying serves the interest of politics: it is used by and aimed at individuals. Traditionally, the lie concerns particular facts and serves specific political ends. In this sense the lie works within political history and is subordinated to particular political purposes. But over time a fundamental change takes place. The lie is now aimed at facts everyone knows; it deceives not only particular individuals but also everyone in society (including the liars themselves); and it is aimed not at particular facts but at the entire framework of factuality as such. The lie moves out of its subordinate position, in other words, to become an absolute framework in which nothing but the creation of the lie acts in the world (TP, 252). In this sense, Arendt appears to suggest, there is a certain reversal in the course of political history, in the relation between the lie and politics: if the traditional lie worked within the realm of action defined by politics—and thus served to confirm and further its history as freedom—politics now works within (and serves) the modern lie. At this point the lie is no longer limited to traditional acts of lying by individuals, but rather takes over and exceeds individual intention, driving forward a political process no longer serving purely political ends.

The danger of the lie is thus not a covering over of history but a substitution of its own action (and history) for that of true political beginnings. In totalitarianism, as Arendt suggests in her book *The Origins of Totalitarianism*, the "mass rewriting of history" not only denies the history of the past but also moves forward as the creation of an "entirely fictitious world."[8] This world is made to be fictitious both in the sense that its fictions are forced upon reality and in the sense that through "organized" propaganda and terror it eliminates the capacity for human beings to act and produces a world of marionettes acting in entirely predictable and mechanical ways. The action of lying is thus not simply a covering over of reality (as in traditional deception) but a replacement of reality altogether with the fiction of an overarching lie:

> All these lies, whether their authors know it or not, harbor an element of violence: organized lying always tends to destroy whatever it has decided to negate, although only totalitarian governments have consciously adopted lying as the first step to murder. . . . In other words, the difference between the traditional lie and the modern lie will more often than not amount to the difference between hiding and destroying.[9]

The violence of the modern lie consists in the absolute loss of the reality that it denies. But we could also say that the violence of the lie, in this process, consists in substituting the action of destroying the facts of reality for the action of beginning, replacing a history of beginnings with a history of their total erasure.

The historical newness of the lie, as Arendt describes it—its unfolding as a true history—thus consists in the conversion of the process of political action into the action of this substitution. But how do we understand the historical moment that leads to this kind of usurpation? In Arendt's repeated reference to the outbreak of World War I, she hints at the possibility that this shift takes place when the massive destructiveness of this war—a kind of destruction that, she will say elsewhere, inaugurated a new world of technological violence—is itself denied. The denial of the responsibility for the beginning of the war, which she refers to repeatedly in her examples, may be the first lie, in fact, that leads to this modern world. To understand the nature of the historical progress of the lie we must understand, then, the way in which the violence of war becomes entangled with the violence of its denial. The problem of history in the world of the lie thus ultimately becomes, as I interpret Arendt, the critical question: What does it mean for the historical violence of war to become the history of the violence of the lie?

LYING AND WAR

It is this question that, I will suggest, lies at the heart of Arendt's analysis of the Vietnam War. "Lying in Politics" is a response to Daniel Ellsberg's release of the so-called Pentagon Papers, the "top-secret" history of the decision-making processes in the war that was leaked to the *New York Times* in 1971 at the height of the conflict, which created shock waves throughout the public sphere because of their revelation of the systematic and pervasive use of lies on all levels in the war. As Arendt notes, this lying involved, among other things, "the phony body counts of the 'search-and-destroy' missions, the doctored after-damage reports of the air force, and the 'progress' reports to Washington from the field written by subordinates who knew that their performance would be evaluated by their own reports,"[10] among other kinds of deception. For Arendt, it is the centrality of deception (as opposed to error or illusion) that constitutes the major lesson of the Pentagon Papers: the centrality of deception as not only a secondary but also a fundamental factor in the decision-making process shaping the development of the war:

> The Pentagon Papers . . . tell different stories, teach different lessons to different readers. . . . But most readers have now agreed that the basic issue raised by the papers is deception. . . . The famous credibility gap . . . has suddenly opened up into an abyss. The quicksand of lying statements of all sorts, deceptions as well as self-deceptions, is apt to engulf any reader who wishes to probe this material, which, unhappily, he must recognize as the infrastructure of nearly a decade of United States foreign and domestic policy. (LP, 3–4)

To the extent that deception appears in the war, it appears not only as a secondary matter in a larger political and military process—a "gap" between the public version of the war and its political realities—but as an "abyss" that opens up within the infrastructure of the policymaking process itself. Drawing on the currently popular description of the war as a quagmire in her own figure of the "quicksand" of lying statements, Arendt shifts the center of action from the actual process of military engagement—presented, in the quagmire model, as a well-intentioned but misguided step-by-step entrance into the conflict—to the process of lying itself, which thus usurps the place of politics as the fundamental action driving the decision-making process of the war.

The process of deception in the war, as Arendt analyses it, can thus be understood as a new, nontotalitarian version of the *modern* lie. This "more recent variet[y]" of lying she refers to specifically as "image-making" (LP, 8), which involves two different, but apparently related, kinds of images: those that change or distort the facts (the images disseminated by the mass media describing the war) and those that guide the war-making decisions themselves. Both kinds of image-making are part of a new phenomenon, and Arendt seems to be touching, quite farsightedly here, on the specificity of a world that is dominated by the mass media. I will suggest, however, that while both kinds of image-making are new, the essential feature that appears to constitute the image as a form of the modern lie is the way in which the image-making involved with the selling of the war is transformed into the image-making that guides the decision-making process itself. It is in the transformative process that takes place *between* the two kinds of image-making, in other words, that the war is not only *hidden as a fact* but also *created as a history*.

We can discern this dynamic relation between the images in Arendt's first description of the two kinds of image-making, that of the "public relations managers" and that of the "problem-solvers." On one hand, Arendt tells us, are the "public relations managers" who "learned their trade from the inventiveness of Madison Avenue," and believe that half of politics is "image-making" and the other half the art of making people believe in the images (LP, 7–9). These image-makers thus *make images*, in effect, to *sell the war*. The problem-solvers, on the other hand, are intellectuals and game theorists who were brought to Washington to calculate scenarios with "game theories and systems analyses" in order to solve the "problems" of foreign policy (LP, 9–10). The problem-solvers, who are "different from ordinary image-makers," are striking because they lie, "not so much for their country— certainly not for their country's survival, which was never at stake—as for its image" (LP, 11). The problem-solvers thus lie, in other words, *in the service of* an image. Arendt's description of the structure of image-making at the heart of the war, as I interpret her argument, thus seems to operate around a reversal that repeats, somewhat differently, the one that governed the transformation from the traditional to the modern lie: if the public relations managers *make images to sell the war*, the problem-solvers *make war to sustain an image*. The war is thus created and sustained, Arendt seems to suggest, for the production of its own image.

Arendt's analysis of the progress of the war in terms of its shifting goals can indeed be understood as a reflection on the way in which the images that sell the war come to take over the decision-making process that guides it. Since "nearly all decisions in this disastrous enterprise were made in full cognizance of the fact that they probably could not be carried out" (LP, 14), Arendt notes, the goals had constantly to be altered. At first these shifts involve the way in which the war is presented to the public. For example, the goal of the war is described originally as "seeing that the people of South Vietnam are permitted to determine their future" but also "assisting the country to win their contest against the . . . Communist conspiracy" (LP, 14). As the war worsens, however, the image-making is not only aimed at convincing the public to support the war but is also incorporated into the conception of the war itself as a kind of image-making process:

> From 1965 on, the notion of a clear-cut victory receded into the background and the objective became "to convince the enemy that *he* could not win" . . . . Since the enemy remained unconvinced, the next goal appeared: "to avoid a humiliating defeat"—as though the hallmark of a defeat in war were mere humiliation. What the Pentagon papers report is the haunting fear of the impact of defeat, not on the welfare of the nation, but on the *reputation* of the United States and its President. (LP, 15)

What emerges as the war grows more difficult—and the goals themselves become less reality-oriented—is not a decision-making process concerning the winning of an actual war but the creation of an "image of omnipotence" that ultimately appears to drive the entire process:

> "To convince the world"; to "demonstrate that U.S. was a 'good doctor' willing to keep promises, be tough, take risks, get bloodied and hurt the enemy badly" . . . to keep intact an image of omnipotence, "our worldwide position of leadership" . . . in short to "*behave* like" the "greatest power in the world" for no other reason than to convince the world of this "simple fact" . . . this was the only permanent goal that, with the beginning of the Johnson administration, pushed into the background all other goals and theories. (LP, 17)

What lies behind the decision-making process is not, as one might expect, an adjustment to events but rather the production of, and adherence to, an "image of omnipotence" that increases in dominance, paradoxically, as true power is lost.

It might seem that the image of omnipotence could itself operate as another traditional form of the lie created in the service of wielding additional power. From this point of view it would remain part of what is ultimately a military and political process in which the image would serve as a traditional political tool. But Arendt argues that the creation of the image of omnipotence actually *undermines* power and puts itself in its place:

> The ultimate aim was neither power nor profit. Nor was it even influence in the world in order to serve particular, tangible interests for the sake of which prestige, an image of the "greatest power in the world," was needed and purposefully used. The goal was now the image itself, as is manifest in the very language of the problem-solvers, with their "scenarios" and "audiences," borrowed from the theater. . . . Image-making as global policy—not world conquest, but victory in the battle "to win the people's minds"—is indeed something new in the huge arsenal of human follies recorded in history. (LP, 17–18)

The "image of omnipotence" has, in fact, no relation to actual power or any other interest to which it might be subordinated, but rather becomes the principle in itself that subordinates all other realities to it. And this is what then constitutes it, paradoxically, as "new" (the hallmark of all true political action): that political decision making would not serve as a true action but as the action of creating an image that empties this process of any power except that of the image itself.

The "image of omnipotence," then, is not created in this war in order to wield more power—as it might be, says Arendt, in "a third-rate nation always apt to boast in order to compensate for the real thing"—but operates in spite of its actual effect of undermining effectiveness in the real world. Wishing to show "how considerable were the chances for a global policy that was then gambled away in the cause of image-making and winning people's minds" (LP, 28–29), Arendt notes two incidents revealed in the Pentagon Papers, the first involving Ho Chi Minh, who had written President Truman in 1945 and 1946 to request support from the United States, and the second involving Mao Tse-tung and Chou En-Lai, who in January 1945 had approached President Roosevelt "trying to establish relations with the United States in order to avoid total dependence on the Soviet Union" (LP, 20). Both overtures were ignored because, as Arendt cites one scholar on the China incident, they "contradicted the image of monolithic Communism directed from Moscow" (LP, 29), an image that would, presumably, be necessary to sustain the converse image of an omnipotent United States winning over a monolithic antithetical power. The creation of the image of omnipotence thus involves the undoing of actual power.

The sustaining of the image is, in this manner, tied to what Arendt calls the process of "defactualization" at the heart of the war by which the decision-making process simultaneously loses its grounding in reality and becomes unable to observe the loss of its own ground. The Vietnam War is, she argues, a war whose very genesis and history serve the establishment of what Arendt calls an entirely "defactualized world" (LP, 36).

HISTORY OF THE IMAGE

What kind of history (and what kind of witness) is possible in the movement toward an entirely defactualized world? Arendt's description of the transformation of the image from the tool to the framework of the decision-making process seems to involve a machinelike mechanism that makes reflection (and truly historical action) increasingly unlikely. Arendt indeed describes a process in which both aspects of the image-making activity have already been essentially cut off from reality. Thus, she explains, the attempt to sell the war becomes, for the image-makers, a battle in which the war is displaced onto the selling process: in thinking of the image-making process as "the battle for people's minds" (LP, 35) the public relations managers essentially allow the image-making itself to take on the properties of the war. The war, for the public relations managers, thus disappears into the image as advertising the war becomes the primary site of the action.

On the other hand, in the case of the problem-solvers (those who lie for the image), the image-making has left the realm of deception and self-deception entirely, since "disregard of reality was inherent in the policies and goals themselves" (LP, 42). *The war itself*, for these policymakers, *has taken on the properties of image-making*. In this quasi-mechanical manner the world and the war thus come to sustain the image that empties this world of any true political significance and ultimately serves only the image's own ongoing and ruthless perpetuation. "One sometimes has the impression," Arendt says, "that a computer, rather than 'decision-makers,' had been let loose in Southeast Asia" (LP, 37). The violent history of the war becomes, in this process, subordinated to the violent historical unfolding of the image (LP, 35).[11]

It is the unfolding movement of this self-erasing image that seems to mark the war *as* an event—a new event—within the larger context of the modern lie. The new aspect of the lie as image-making can itself be traced back, in fact, to an earlier event in history that Arendt will go on to describe. Thus the problem-solvers, Arendt says, were preceded by the Cold War ideologists who had once been Communists and needed a "new ideology to explain and reliably foretell the course of history" (LP, 39). The "sheer ignorance of facts" in this process produced the "theories" of the younger generation (the problem-solvers) that "shield[ed] men from the impact of reality" (LP, 40). And this history—a history not of *facts* but of *defactualization*—

has a beginning in the occurrence of a specific event that is a crucial event in history but also an event in the history of the modern lie:

> There are historians today who maintain that Truman dropped the bomb on Hiroshima in order to scare the Russians out of Eastern Europe (with the result we know). If this is true, as it might well be, then we may trace back the earliest beginnings of the disregard for the actual consequences of action in favor of some ulterior calculated aim to the fateful war crime that ended the last world war. (LP, 43)

At the "earliest beginnings" of defactualization—at the beginning, Arendt implies, of the kind of image-making that usurps the decision-making process in the Vietnam War—is a single and inaugurating act, the decision to drop the atomic bomb. If this decision is the beginning of a new mode of the modern lie, however, of image-making of the kind she has analyzed in the war, then the "action" of this decision (and its violent consequences) as a "beginning" is subordinated to the image it creates. Rather than taking place as a historical event that provides a framework in which the modern lie will develop, the dropping of the bomb (within the logic of Arendt's analysis) converts the frame of political and historical events into the framework of the lie's own self-generation.

The dropping of the bomb, as I would expand on what I discern in Arendt's argument, would not be meant to wield real power but rather to create the image of power, an event that replaces itself with its own image. The bomb is not only the "beginning" of the nuclear age but also the beginning of a certain mode of image-making, a beginning that erases itself as such in this very process. This is particularly striking in the case of the bomb, since as actual, technological power the bomb would seem to embody precisely the omnipotence it would represent as image. Yet this technologically destructive power (and its political potential) is instantly transferred into the image-making that subordinates its present, factual reality (including the reality of its destruction) to the image of a future omnipotence ultimately related only to its power to destroy itself as a fact. The bomb is not dropped in order to wield power that would allow for victory, but rather for the "pursuit of a mere image of omnipotence" that lies in the future (LP, 39).

And yet, it would seem, this "image" of itself is also an actual visual image, insofar as the bomb, in its technological function, is associated with the production of a blinding light (it is often compared to a sun) as well as an image that represents its power, the "image of omnipotence" in the shape of the "mushroom cloud" in which the explosive power of the bomb appears. The bomb thus posits its own image as something that—like the modern lie—is seen and not seen at the same time. The decision to drop the bomb, we could say—which is, or starts as, a true form of action—is covered over, or erased, by the power of the image produced in the actual falling of the bomb, the "mushroom cloud" that gives the falling of the bomb a kind of inevitability (and becomes the term used to make future wars seem inevitable rather than acts of decision making). The erasure of the act of decision making (the process by which a true decision took place) in the dropping of the bomb— the way in which the decision is erased by the image—could be considered the creation of a new kind of fact, one that erases itself in its own production, and in so doing moves forward toward a blinding future. The beginning— and hence futurity—constituted by the "decision" to drop the bomb thus becomes the future "of the image," a history determined by a technological image-making power that determines the future as an explosion annihilating both past and future history.[12]

The end of World War II is ultimately the beginning of the image, a dark (or blindingly light) doubling, perhaps, of the historical process encapsulated at the end of *The Origins of Totalitarianism* in Arendt's claim that "every end in history necessarily contains a new beginning."[13] The history of the lie, in its new form as the history of the image, would be a history constituted by its own erasure. And this is also how we would have to understand its violence: not only as the actual destruction made possible by the bomb but also as the means by which destruction and violence are made, in their very appearance, inaccessible as knowledge. This is indeed the absolute destruction of fact that Arendt names in the first section of "Lying in Politics" as another mode of omnipotence: "[The destruction of facts] can be done only through radical destruction. . . . [T]he power to achieve it would have to amount to omnipotence . . . to wield power over the libraries and archives of all countries of the earth" (LP, 13).

EXPLOSIVE HISTORIES

If the dropping of the bomb is the advent of the image, however, Arendt's own writing also bears witness to the trace of another explosion, an explosion, moreover, associated with an exemplary fact. This fact—mentioned in the quotation from "Truth and Politics" with which we began—also marks the beginning of a war and is repeated four times in the essay as representative of both the coerciveness of facts and of their fragility: "the fact that on the night of August 4, 1914, German troops crossed the frontier of Belgium." In *The Origins of Totalitarianism*, however, this fact has a complicated structure, since it marks, as it turns out, the transition from the pretotalitarian to the totalitarian world and opens the famous chapter ("The

Decline of the Nation State and the End of the Rights of Man") that pivots between them:

> It is almost impossible even now to describe what actually happened in Europe on August 4, 1914. The days before and the days after the first World War are separated not like the end of an old and the beginning of a new period, but like the day before and the day after an explosion. Yet this figure of speech is as inaccurate as are all others, because the quiet of sorrow which settles down after a catastrophe has never come to pass. The first explosion seems to have touched off a chain reaction in which we have been caught ever since and which nobody seems to be able to stop. . . . Every event had the finality of a last judgment, a judgment that was passed neither by God nor by the devil, but looked rather like the expression of some unredeemably stupid fatality.[14]

The "fact" (which is also a date) of August 4, 1914, derives from an event of a special kind, a transitional event between two worlds that constitutes a radical change in political history, from the post-Revolutionary world to the world in which much of European politics was ultimately subordinated to the totalitarian movements. As such it heralds something new in history, although, Arendt notes, it is not the newness of a beginning but rather of an "explosion," a gap in time that does not produce a future but rather appears to annihilate it. Indeed, the atomic nature of the explosion (related to a chain reaction) suggests, on a figural level, a link between this historical event marking the beginning of World War I and the literal event of explosion that marks the end of World War II, a chain of explosions in which the beginnings and the ends are equally destructive and seem to produce a history constituted only as the repeated erasure of the histories that precede them.

The explosion of August 4, 1914, indeed marks a transition, specifically, between the world of the traditional lie and the world of the modern lie. As such, the explosion is precisely the advent of the modern lie as a historical event, but an event of a new kind: an event heralding the possibility of its total erasure. The history of explosions would thus constitute the historical unfolding of the modern lie as a repetition of erasures, each both eliminated and passed on by the one that follows.

The figure of explosion that Arendt uses here, however, also delineates this repetitive history in its *difference from* the pure mechanicity and determination of the bomb, insofar as it reverses the order of explosion and chain reaction: "Yet this figure of speech is as inaccurate as are all others, because the quiet of sorrow which settles down after a catastrophe has never come to pass. The first explosion seems to have touched off a chain reaction in which we have been caught ever since and which nobody seems able to stop." Whereas in an ordinary, single event of atomic explosion the chain reaction would precede the explosion, here the explosion precedes the chain reaction, which then causes another explosion and another into the future. The explosion, that is, does not take place except insofar as it creates another one, a figure not so much of purely mechanical processes as of a repetition of explosions whose impact always lies in the future of explosions to come. If the advent of the modern lie, in history, is also the advent of history's erasure (as event), this reversal suggests that this erasure never quite occurs, that it is only half erased and transmitted to the future where it leaves its traces in the violent imprint (and in the technology associated with it) that accompanies the bomb. In Arendt's text, then, the violent and blinding light of the bomb, *as an image*, bears with it the *trace of a figure* that is passed on through the very process of its (partial) erasure.[15] The distinction between the image and its figure would permit, here, a nonmechanistic, nondeterministic historicity of the modern lie—and the possibility of its witness—to begin to emerge.

THE POSSIBILITY OF WITNESS

It is the trace of this self-erasure of the historical fact that Daniel Ellsberg might indeed be understood as describing when he says, in *Papers on the War*, that he leaked the Pentagon Papers in order to reveal an "invisible war"[16]—not only a war that was invisible to the public but also, perhaps, a war constituted by its self-elimination as a traditional fact. Ellsberg's revelation of the Pentagon Papers is in fact not the revelation of a simple secret, as Arendt notes at the end of her essay:

> What calls for further close and detailed study is the fact, much commented on, that the Pentagon papers revealed little significant news that was not available to the average reader of dailies and weeklies; nor are there any arguments, pro or con, in the "History of the U.S. Decision-Making Process on Vietnam Policy" that have not been debated publicly for years in magazines, television shows, and radio broadcasts. (LP, 45)

While Arendt emphasizes the availability of the facts because she wishes to insist on the importance of a free press, I believe that her recognition that the Pentagon Papers do not reveal new facts points to a reinterpretation of the way in which the media could be understood as working in their disclosure. If the Pentagon Papers have the force of a revelation, it cannot be because they reveal any facts that are not known (including the facts of the lies themselves) but rather because they produce, from within the very medium of the image (the public press), the force of an explosion that transmits and makes legible the explosion of the fact in the modern world. It is, perhaps, the performance of a kind of *explosion of the frame* of the media through the very media that create this frame.[17]

Ellsberg himself describes his decision to leak the Pentagon Papers not in terms of revelation or truth but in terms of the breaking of a promise—the breaking of the secrecy oath that, in an essay on the subject, he identifies as a promise to lie.[18] Ellsberg's decision is a peculiar kind of speech act: not a promise—a central kind of political action in Arendt's work—but the *breaking of a promise to lie*. This new kind of action would have to be understood as an action that forgoes the possibility of straightforward truth-telling yet serves, nonetheless, as a form of political witness. What occurs here is not the telling of truth, that is, but the testimony to erasure: the exposure, in Ellsberg's words, of an "enigma,"[19] the enigma of an "invisible war"—that is, a *witness to invisibility*.

In Arendt's response to this witness, I would propose, we may also discern, not so much the truth of the lie's history, but the possible outlines, and performance, of a certain historicity—passing through the beginning of World War I, the end of World War II, the endless war in Vietnam, and a future of wars (and of lies) that Arendt could not know would arise out of the post-Vietnam era but about which she seemed to write so presciently—a historicity that does not submit itself entirely to the absolute violence of the lie. Only by thinking through the possibility of total erasure, Arendt shows us, can we also conceive of the possibility of a decision to witness that itself, as an action, has political and historical consequences—the possibility for a witness from within the world of the lie. In Arendt's own writing, it is at the point at which we discern the radically self-annihilating historicity of the bomb that we may also trace the figure of an explosion not entirely determined by its self-erasure. The trace of this figure would not necessarily be a promise, but might serve, instead, as testimony to the possibility of another history.

CHAPTER FOUR

Disappearing History

SCENES OF TRAUMA IN THE THEATER
OF HUMAN RIGHTS

Ariel Dorfman, *Death and the Maiden*

ARIEL DORFMAN'S 1991 PLAY *Death and the Maiden* is set in the present time in a country that "is probably Chile" but "could be any country that has just departed from a dictatorship" (translation modified).[1] Taking place in a remote beach house primarily on a single night and day, the
play follows the actions of a woman, Paulina, who has been tortured by the
previous regime and whose husband, Gerardo, a human rights lawyer, has
just been appointed to head a truth commission established by the new
transitional government. Surprised in the middle of the night by Roberto,
a stranger who has given Gerardo a ride home and returns unexpectedly at
midnight to give Gerardo back his spare tire, Paulina believes she recognizes
the voice and idioms of the man who tortured her while she was blindfolded. She ultimately manages to capture Roberto in the house and stage
a "trial" at gunpoint in which, with the coerced cooperation of her husband, she forces from the stranger a confession, while playing a tape of the
Schubert quartet that was played while she was raped. Unsatisfied by the
"confession," Paulina considers killing him, an act left suspended in the play,
the last scene of which ends in a theater where the Schubert quartet is being
performed and where Paulina believes she sees Roberto (or his ghost) staring
at her in a phantasmatic light.

Written during the transitional government that followed the Pinochet
dictatorship in Chile, and produced for the first time the year before the
appearance of the report by the National Commission on Truth and Reconciliation assigned to document the regime's acts of "disappearing" people,[2]
the play evokes, in its emphasis on documentation and confession, the role
of recovering truth in the return to democracy and human rights.[3] Struc-

tured, moreover, by a series of stagings—Roberto plays the role of a helpful neighbor to Gerardo; Paulina stages the torture and trial of Roberto;[4] and Gerardo stages a testimonial interview for Paulina—the play specifically links the question of truth to the nature of its appearance, or the role of "performance" in the undoing and reconstitution of justice. At the heart of performance in the play, I will suggest, and specifically in the centrality of a particular kind of performance—the performance of the Schubert quartet, which names the play and serves as a central part of its story—is a struggle between the reappearance of democracy and the disappearance of history, between the reenactment of trauma and the possible performance of a new kind of listening.

RETURN AND DISAPPEARANCE

The play begins with the encounter between two kinds of return: the return home of Gerardo, the human rights lawyer, who meets his wife, Paulina, herself returned years before from her own disappearance and torture. Gerardo clearly represents, in the play, the "return to democracy" that should be enabled by the truth commission he has just been appointed to lead, and in particular the role of human rights law in the appearance of truth.[5] "We will find out [what happened]," Gerardo tells his wife: "Find out everything. . . . We'll publish our conclusions. There will be an official report. What happened will be established objectively, so no one will ever be able to deny it" (DM, 10). But the truth appearing in the report will exclude one particular mode of truth, the truth, precisely, embodied by Paulina's very return:

Paulina: This Commission you're named to. Doesn't it only investigate cases that ended in death?
Gerardo: It's appointed to investigate human rights violations that ended in death or the presumption of death, yes.
Paulina: Only the most serious cases?
Gerardo: The idea is that if we can throw light on the worst crimes, other abuses will come to light.
Paulina: Only the most serious?
Gerardo: Let's say the cases that are beyond—let's say, repair.
Paulina: Beyond repair. Irreparable, huh?
Gerardo: I don't like to talk about this, Paulina. (DM, 9)

The truth of the "disappearances" in the report of the commission excludes, it turns out, the disappearances of those who returned: the living testimony of the disappeared who actually reappear in the new democracy. Echoing the language of the actual Chilean commission that, likewise, focused only on disappeared people who were never recovered or were known to have died, the truth of political disappearance, in the Commission's framework, can be established only as the increasingly distant act of the past.[6] Gerardo's commission in the play, like the report from which it draws its language, thus shuns a mode of truth in which the disappearing lingers on in the return. While the circumstantial reason for this exclusion, in the Chilean context of the play, concerns the continuing presence of the military in post-dictatorial society—and the danger of reprisals, or even another coup, if survivors have the capacity to name their military torturers—the play's unspecified setting extends its significance beyond any particular political limitation.[7] There appears to be a more fundamental problem, in other words, at the heart of Paulina's return.[8] The play allegorizes the emergence of this other mode of return—in the figure of Paulina and in the action of the rest of the play—at the moment of the commission's (and democracy's) reestablishment and reappearance.

Paulina, herself, seems, in her very return, to remain stuck at the site of a disappearing, not simply in a personal psychological sense (although this is what her husband believes and will tell her explicitly),[9] but more importantly in a political sense. Paulina's inability to be inserted into the story being created by the democratic human rights commission—her problematic legal status at this particular transitional site[10]—evokes, oddly, the (in)famous description of the disappeared given by General Rafael Videla, the de facto president of Argentina during their Dirty War, at a press conference where he was confronted with the disappearings and murders. Videla also invokes the language of human rights—though in a "Christian" context—and of democratic principles of legal procedure, with an exception for the case of a disappeared person:

> with a Christian vision of human rights, the vision of life is fundamental, the vision of liberty is important, as is a vision of work, of family, of lifestyle, etc. Argentina attends to human rights with a comprehensive understanding of the term "human rights." But speaking in more concrete terms—because I know you ask me this question not with this comprehensive understanding in mind exemplified by the generic ideal of human rights referred to by the Pope, but rather more concretely as understood in terms of a man who is detained without legal recourse on the one hand, or the man who is disappeared on the other. If that man appeared, well, he would receive treatment X and if his disappearance resulted in the certainty of his death he would

receive treatment Z. But while he is disappeared he cannot receive any special treatment, he is an unknown, he is disappeared, he has no age, he is not present. Neither dead nor alive, he is disappeared.[11]

Videla's use of the term "disappeared" is meant to evade, of course, the true meaning of "disappeared," or to make the referent of the term—the kidnapping, torture, and murder of Argentinean citizens by the military regime—itself disappear in a nicety about legal hypotheticals. But the language of his lie—what Hannah Arendt would call a "modern lie," the lie about facts that everyone knows, the lie that acts in place of true political action, and is thus the public disappearing of facts that appear before everyone's eyes[12]—also introduces the strange reality of a new kind of person, the person without rights, the "rightless" (as Arendt called them)[13] who are suspended between life and legal death. What returns with Paulina, then, is a mode of "disappearing" that cannot simply be incorporated within the language or understanding of the law.[14]

It is, interestingly, the story of a disappearance and return that lies at the heart of the twentieth century's most profound thinking of trauma, Sigmund Freud's notion of "repetition compulsion" published in *Beyond the Pleasure Principle* after World War I.[15] In Freud's famous example of a child playing *fort* and *da* ("gone" and "here") with a spool, Freud first interprets the game as a performance [*Spiel*, both "game" and theatrical performance] in two "acts" [*Akte*]: a disappearance followed by a return that transforms, imaginatively and wishfully, the painful event of the mother's absence into an experience of her returning presence. "This, then, was the complete game," Freud says, "disappearance and return" [*Verschwinden und Wiederkommen*]. Upon closer observation, however, Freud suggests that it is the first act, that of disappearance, that is most often performed as a game in itself, a game that no longer transforms a painful event into a comforting psychological meaning but only repeats the meaningless disappearance in its unassimilable incomprehension. The performance of disappearance, in other words—the throwing of the spool and the repetition of the sound of the "*fort*"—reenacts an event that has not yet been fully understood and that returns, unconsciously, in the child's very gestures and words. Rather than transforming a known, and painful, event into an illusion of pleasure, that is, the game rather repeats an event that recedes from awareness even as it reemerges in the game. The disappearance of the mother thus itself repeatedly *disappears from consciousness* in the very reenactment of the performance.[16]

It is this *disappearance of the event itself*—its retreat from the full consciousness of both individuals and of society[17]—that, I will suggest, is ultimately reenacted in the performances of all three characters in Dorfman's play, beginning with the return of the third character, Roberto, in the middle of the night. In the centrality of performance staged in the play—in Paulina's staging of a scene of torture and "trial," in Gerardo's staging of a scene of testimony, and in the play's own staging of the performance of music as a central prop and figure of performance itself—the play can be said to re-enact the traumatic nature of the *return of disappearance* as it threatens to undo the possibility of truth, and the achievement of justice, at the heart of the returning democracy.

AN UNCONSCIOUS PERFORMANCE

The behavioral reenactment so central to the play can be said to take place not only in Paulina's behavior throughout the play but also, more funda-mentally, in the action of all three characters as they deliver a series of staged performances. These performances, I would suggest, begin with an-other return, the return of the third character, Roberto, in the middle of the night:

> *Someone knocks on the door, first timidly, then more strongly. A lamp is switched on from offstage and is immediately switched off. The knocking on the door gets more insistent. Gerardo comes into the living room in his pajamas from the bedroom.*
> **Gerardo** (*to Paulina, who is offstage*): I'm telling you—nothing is going to—all right, all right, love, I'll be careful.
> . . . .
> *He goes to the door and opens it. Roberto Miranda is outside.*
> **Gerardo:** Oh, it's you. God, you scared the shit out of me.
> **Roberto:** I'm really so sorry for this—intrusion. . . .
> **Gerardo:** You must excuse my . . . —do come in.
> *Roberto enters the house.*
>   It's just that we still haven't got used to it.
> **Roberto:** Used to it?
> **Gerardo:** To democracy. That someone knocks on your door at midnight and it's a friend and not . . . — (*DM*, 12)

Hearing an enigmatic and frightening nighttime knock, Gerardo rapidly turns it into a comforting story, not only of the return of the kindly stranger, but even more grandly, of the return of democracy itself: "We still haven't got used to . . . democracy. That someone knocks on your door at midnight and it's a friend." It is this immediate transformation of the sound into a recognizable sign that initiates a conversation between Roberto and Gerardo that, while focused on the problem of truth—the possibility of the discovery and revelation of the names of the perpetrators in Gerardo's new truth commission—turns into an odd performance in which the two men systematically cite each other's words and even exchange positions on whether or not the truth will be fully revealed.[18] The theatrical context of this performance is emphasized by the presence of an audience, Paulina, who listens fearfully from the next room, clearly frightened by Gerardo's conversation with the stranger. Rather than expressing an opinion or perspective on the nature of democracy and truth, then, Gerardo appears to be engaged in an unconscious production of a *story of return* that never examines the truth of its own performance.[19]

It is, notably, not in direct relation to Roberto, but in response to the performance she secretly overhears, that Paulina shortly thereafter initiates her own action in the play, transforming herself from audience to actor.[20] Paulina sneaks into the living room in the middle of the night, ties up Roberto as he sleeps on the couch (invited to stay by Gerardo), and wakes him the next morning with a gun in his face and the sound of Schubert on the cassette recorder:

Paulina: Good morning Doctor . . . Miranda, isn't it?

. . . .

I took this out of your car—I took the liberty—what if we listen to some Schubert while I make breakfast . . . , Doctor? *Death and the Maiden*?

. . . .

D'you know how long it's been since I last listened to this quartet? If it's on the radio, I turn it off. . . . I always pray [people] won't put on Schubert. One night . . . our hostess happened to put Schubert on. . . . I felt extremely ill right then and there . . . so we left them there listening to Schubert and nobody knew what had made me ill. . . .

. . . .

Is this the very cassette [that you played for me], Doctor, or do you buy a new one every year to keep the sound pure? (*DM*, 19–22, translation modified)[21]

Whereas Gerardo interprets the sound of the knock as a sign—the sign of a returning democracy—Paulina apparently experiences the sound of Roberto's voice as a returning referent: the return of the past in the form of her torturer. Emerging as a critical response to Gerardo's conversation, Paulina's behavior first appears as a questioning of the somewhat naïve assumptions of Gerardo's (somewhat self-serving) story.[22] Indeed, as the action continues and Paulina attempts to re-create, with Roberto, the torture that she apparently suffered while listening to Schubert, Paulina appears to refer directly to her own experience, which she says she remembers through Roberto's voice and which she re-creates, in a male voice, in occasional citations of her torturer's words: "'Give her a bit more. This bitch can take a bit more. Give it to her'" (DM, 23). Yet Paulina, blindfolded during her own torture, does not refer to this torture directly but rather re-creates a scene dominated by sound—the sound of Roberto's voice, the sound of her own voice as she repeats his, the sound of the Schubert performed before and played again in this scene. This soundscape, which is directed at another audience, Gerardo, does not elicit a recognition of truth but only reproduces Paulina's exclusion from the site of truth: in Roberto's proclamations of innocence and in Gerardo's claims that Paulina cannot know what she has only heard. "A vague memory of someone's voice is not proof of anything, Paulina," Gerardo scolds her, "it is not incontrovertible" (DM, 23).

Rather than simply representing two different but equally valid perceptions of the truth, then—that Roberto is either a returning neighbor or a returning torturer, that he represents either the returning democracy or the returning (dictatorial) past—Gerardo and Paulina may be said to be involved, together, in an *unconscious reenactment* in which the very notion of directly accessible truth is itself undermined by the performance in which it is staged. This performance also underlies, I would suggest, Gerardo's and Paulina's dilemma surrounding the possibility of achieving justice for the victims of the dictatorship. Thus Gerardo, hoping to save democracy, tells Roberto that he believes the death penalty "never solved any[thing]"(DM, 16), hence preferring the path of the law, whereas Paulina, unable to gain access to this law, points a gun at Roberto and threatens to kill him if he doesn't "confess" (DM 41, 42). Roberto himself interprets these positions in a theatrical manner when he complains to Gerardo—who has been convinced by Paulina to act as a "lawyer" for Roberto and make him "confess"—that the husband and wife are playing distinctive "roles": "From the beginning you've been conspiring with her. She plays the bad guy and you play the good guy and— . . . [You're] [p]laying roles [*repartiéndose los roles*], she's bad, you're good, to see if you can get me to confess" (DM, 47, and in the Spanish original, *La Muerte y La Doncella, MD*, 62). Although Roberto is not entirely correct in his interpretation—he believes that the roles are part of an "interrogation" that will inevitably end with his death—he is also not entirely incorrect, in that the enactment of the "trial" is also a reenactment of Paulina's torture, and her conscious intention to reveal the truth is mixed in with other not fully conscious dimensions of performance on both Paulina's and Gerardo's (and, we might add, Roberto's) parts. From the moment of Roberto's arrival, we might say, the terms of their discourse—the values of "truth," "justice" and "democracy" as well as "rights" and "humanitarianism" as espoused by Gerardo and Roberto, and the need for a "trial" and "confession" expressed by Paulina—are mixed in uncomfortably with the language of torture (also a language of "confession") as well as with the possibility of role-playing, both conscious and unconscious.

In the impasses of truth and justice established in the play—between a law that does not provide truth or justice,[23] and an act of revenge that threatens the reestablishment of the law—the play thus seems to pose a dilemma, one in which audiences and critics have generally responded either by pointing to the impossibility of a solution or by taking sides with Gerardo or Paulina.[24] But the repeated playing of the Schubert quartet—both inside the action and outside the action in the play's title; first introduced through the tape recorder by Paulina and then played offstage in act 2, as a setting for the ongoing action; and finally brought back onstage in a "live" performance at the end—suggests that the performances of the three characters in the opening act(s) of the play are themselves bound up with the repetition of an *earlier mode of performance* that, not exactly visible to the characters or audience, returns onstage through the characters' reenactments. It is a specific kind of performance, then, returning from the past, that continually disappears even as it reemerges, that obliterates its own history even as it becomes an object of confession and revenge.

A VIOLATED EAR

Indeed, the Schubert quartet introduced by Paulina has a unique status in the role-playing and stagings that dominate the interaction among the three characters. For the music of Schubert takes place not only as *part of* the various reenactments on the stage. The quartet is also, *itself*, a very specific kind of performance: the performance of music that is replayed on the tape recorder and played "live" in the final scene of the drama. The music in the play, I would argue, is thus not only a prop in the characters' performances but also a theatrical symbol or figure that reflects on *the nature of performance itself*. The playing of Schubert throughout *Death and the Maiden* can be said to provide an implicit reflection, a kind of metacommentary, on the nature of the various performances that govern the behavior of all three characters in the play, both past and present (and, of course, a commentary on the performance of Dorfman's play as well). The quartet is, moreover, in this context, a musical presentation that, as we shall see, equally serves as evidence for Paulina's past and seems to deny the certainty of its occurrence. It is in the very actions of playing and listening, then, in the scenes of a musical performance that both calls for and resists being heard, that we can trace the emergence of a history that repeatedly returns and disappears.

This past is, in fact, first directly designated by Paulina in terms of the act of playing music. When, in the first act, Gerardo awakens in shock to the scene of Paulina holding Roberto at gunpoint with the Schubert playing in the background, Paulina responds to her husband's demand for an explanation by identifying Roberto not in direct reference to torture but rather in terms of the music itself:

Gerardo: What the hell is going on here, what kind of madness is—
Paulina: It's him.
. . .
Gerardo: Who?
Paulina: It's the doctor.
Gerardo: What doctor?
Paulina: The doctor who played Schubert.
Gerardo: The doctor who played Schubert.
Paulina: That doctor. (*DM*, 22)

Rather than identifying Roberto as her "torturer," Paulina names him in terms of a certain kind of performance: "the doctor who played Schubert [*el que tocaba Schubert*]" (*DM*, 22; *MD*, 36). While the substitution of the music for the direct reference to torture might seem to act as a circumlocution, it can also be understood, differently, to designate the music as itself identified with the torture, not only serving as a *setting for* torture but also *constitutive of* its very nature. The verb *tocar*, used here to describe Roberto's actions (*el que tocaba Schubert* [the one who played Schubert]), immediately denotes the use of a tape recorder, recalling Paulina's first reference to the tape-playing when she addresses Roberto, "Is this the very cassette [that you played for me], Doctor . . . ? [¿*Es la misma que usted me tocó, doctor . . . ?*]" (*DM*, 22; *MD*, 35). The verb for "playing" (*tocar*) thus links the tape-playing of the present moment (as Paulina holds Roberto at gunpoint) with the tape-playing of the past (when Paulina was presumably held by Roberto by force, and raped while the music was played). But the verb *tocar* also means "performance" in a broader sense, and thus alludes to the torture itself as a kind of performance that not only plays music in the background but also performs along with it in an intricate and disturbing manner. The ambiguity of the verb *tocar*, as both tape-playing and performing, consequently suggests a subtle confusion of the kinds of performance constituted by the playing of a quartet and the various forms of violence inflicted upon Paulina.[25] And this confusion is also inherent in the title of the quartet, *Death and the Maiden*, which seems to refer not only to the Schubert but also to the interactions between the torturer (Death) and his victim (the Maiden). Roberto's playing of the *Death and the Maiden* quartet and Paulina's forced listening to it thus become part of what constitutes the rape and pain of torture, *a violence to the ear* that accompanies the physical violence imposed upon her body and is central to the scene of torture as a whole.[26]

That the music is part of the torture is also indicated by the way in which it affects Paulina's body, an effect that serves as one form of evidence of her past experience. But this evidence of the scene of torture, of forced listening during painful physical experimentation and rape, occurs in the form of a peculiar return, the return of the experience, as we recall from the scene between Paulina and Roberto cited above, in Paulina's *inability to listen*:

> **Paulina** (to Roberto): D'you know how long it's been since I last listened
> to this quartet? If it's on the radio, I turn it off. . . . I always pray
> [people] won't put on Schubert. One night . . . our hostess hap-
> pened to put Schubert on . . . I felt extremely ill right then and
> there and Gerardo had to take me home. . . . (*DM*, 21)

While an ordinary performance of Schubert would make Paulina desire to hear more (as Schubert is in fact, she tells Roberto, her "favorite composer" [*DM*, 21]), the torture has created an *inability to listen*, a physiological repugnance whenever the music is played. And this inability to listen is not limited to Paulina's inability to listen to the music used during her torture. It seems to spread to others, to be bound up, indeed, with the inability of her husband to listen to her speak:

> **Paulina**: So when I heard his voice, I thought the only thing I want is to
> have him raped, have someone fuck him, that's what I thought,
> that he should know just once what it is to . . . And as I can't
> rape—I thought that it was a sentence that you would have to
> carry out.
> **Gerardo**: Don't go on, Paulina. (*DM*, 40)[27]

If for Paulina the inability to listen to the Schubert is the return of the experience of torture, the referent that is absolutely real for her, for Gerardo, on the other hand, Paulina's mode of responding to music only produces a desire not to listen to Paulina and a disbelief in the veracity of her words.

The forced listening at the heart of the performance of the scene of torture returns, therefore, as an inability to listen that makes the evidence of the torture inaccessible as a mode of truth.[28]

Paulina's attempt to force Roberto to listen to the tape of Schubert, therefore—during which Roberto also becomes a captive audience to her narration of parts of her past—is not only Paulina's attempt to reverse and control her experience, but also a means of guaranteeing the truth, by linking the scene of performance—of music, of actions, of "trial" and "torture"—to a confession:

> **Paulina** [to Gerardo]: And you know . . . the only thing I really want? . . .
> I want him to confess. I want him to sit in front of that cassette recorder and tell me what he did—not just to me, everything, to everybody. . . . (DM, 41)

The cassette recorder, as the site of a confession, would presumably convert the music, also played on a cassette, into a form of evidence, the evidence of its own role in the event of torture. Paulina's performance thus aims not only at reversing the power relations between Roberto and herself but also at converting the act of performance—as it is bound up with the music— from an event that cannot be heard into a story that can be told, a story, that is, to which others will be able to listen. The struggle with truth in the play thus emerges from a particular kind of event that is specific to the context of the play but resonates, symbolically, beyond it: an event or mode of action that is, peculiarly, constituted by the undoing of its transmission, a performance that appears to inscribe, within in it, the impossibility of listening to the story of its occurrence.[29]

THE BETRAYAL OF LISTENING

That the event of torture is linked inherently to the problem of listening and performing is made clearer by the climactic scene in which the story of Paulina's torture is finally told, a scene that is itself an intricate and complex scene of staging and performance. After hours of struggle with both Roberto and her husband, Paulina has convinced her husband to play the role of Roberto's "lawyer," who convinces Roberto to provide a taped and written "confession" in order to be freed (as Paulina has promised). Meanwhile Gerardo, finally professing a desire to listen to Paulina, has offered to provide a taped session for her as well, and convinces her to tell the story of her torture—which she has never fully told to Gerardo—"just as if you were sitting in front of the Commission" (DM, 57). The two stories are provided in an overlapping sequence in which the music of Death and the Maiden is played from somewhere offstage. The story of Paulina's torture is thus offered as a moment of truth that is equally a moment of carefully and consciously constructed stagings that offer the truth as intimately bound up with the nature of its performance.

This performance does not, as one might expect, undermine the sense of veracity transmitted by the narration: the continuity between Paulina's words, which begin the story, and Roberto's words, which continue it, appear to provide a convincing account of the brutal fact of Paulina's rape and torture. But this narrative continuity, notably, takes place in a sequence in which Paulina's words break off, and Roberto's words take over, drowning out Paulina's voice at the very moment that she describes the beginning of Roberto's actions in the past. The fading away of Paulina's narrative occurs, moreover, just as she refers to the first time she heard, during her captivity, the music of Schubert:

> Paulina: I met Doctor Miranda for the first time three days [after my
> abduction] when . . . That's when I met Doctor Miranda.
> *The lights go down further and Paulina's voice continues in the darkness,*
> *only the cassette recorder lit by the light of the moon.*
> At first, I thought he would save me. He was so soft, so—nice,
> after what the others had done to me. And then, all of a sudden,
> I heard a Schubert quartet. There is no way of describing what
> it means to hear that wonderful music in the darkness when you
> haven't eaten for the last three days, when your body is falling
> apart, when . . .
> *In the darkness, we hear Roberto's voice overlapping with Paulina's and the*
> *second movement of* Death and the Maiden.
> Roberto's voice: I would put on the music because it helped me in my role,
> the role of good guy, as they call it, I would put on Schubert
> because it was a way of gaining the prisoners' trust.[30] (*DM*, 58)

The power of this story, as it emerges through Paulina and Roberto, consists not simply in the reference of their words to the acts at the time of Paulina's detention: to Paulina's starvation, her hope at the sound of the music, and Roberto's cynical use of the music to gain her trust. The breaking off of Paulina's narrative in the dark and the transition to the words of Roberto, as the music comes up over the scene, also *reenacts* the events that are being told, and does so in the disappearance of Paulina's words behind the voice of Roberto. Although Paulina keeps speaking, her words cannot be heard—we are unable to listen to them—just as she describes how the music to which she originally listened with pleasure is turned into a tool for her torture.

This music, played offstage and hovering over the present scene of Paulina's testimony and Roberto's confession, thus reenacts the scene of torture as the very moment when Paulina begins to lose her ability to listen, which is also the moment when she will lose the ability to tell: that is, when she will lose the possibility of finding an audience able to hear in its turn.[31]

This moment when Paulina loses her ability to listen to Schubert is itself enacted as something not fully grasped by Paulina, as the very break in the sentence as she describes her act of listening: "There is no way of describing what it means to hear [*escuchar*, to listen to] that wonderful music in the darkness" (*DM*, 58; *MD*, 71).[32] As Roberto continues to tell the story in his confession, he describes this moment of listening by Paulina from his own perspective: "I would put on the music because it helped me in my role, the role of good guy, as they call it, I would put on Schubert because it was a way of gaining the prisoners' trust."[33] Repeating the notion of role-playing that he has used earlier in his accusations of Gerardo, Roberto claims that the music is simply part of his performance of a "role," "the role of good guy [*el rol del bueno*]" (*DM*, 58; *MD*, 71). The *listening* of Paulina, that is, when she first meets the doctor and hears the Schubert quartet, *has already become part of the performance of Roberto*, a performance he will later refer to as a "game [*juego*]" (*DM*, 59; *MD*, 73). What Paulina cannot grasp, that is, is that the agency and pleasure of her listening have already, at the very first moment of her encounter with her torturer, been inscribed as actions in *another's* cruel performance. The music will thus lose its power to evoke and refer to Paulina's own will and desire and, from that point on, evoke and refer itself only to the desire and power of Roberto, and to the missed moment of her inscription in his game. Paulina's very words *about* the music, in her scene of testimony, will likewise elicit and become lost in the narration by Roberto.

The experience of Paulina hearing the music during her detention, is thus, we might say, the suffering of a kind of betrayal, but one that operates in a specific and peculiar fashion.[34] While Paulina originally believes that Roberto is there (as a doctor, as "kind," and as a player of Schubert) to "save her," he turns out to be another torturer who uses his appearance of kindness as a tool of cynical seduction. But what Paulina experiences as not being saved, is, in Roberto's terms, precisely his way of "saving" a prisoner:

> Roberto: You've got to believe it was a way of alleviating the prisoners' suffering. Not only the music, but everything else I did . . .
>
> . . . .
>
> The prisoners were dying on them, they told me, they needed

someone to help care for them. . . . The real real truth, it was for
humanitarian reasons . . . I thought . . . they still have the right to
some form of medical attention. . . .

. . . .

[N]ot one ever died on me, not one of the women, not one of the
men. (*DM*, 58–60)[35]

Roberto claims that he accepted the job with the prisoners as a way of saving them from death: "The prisoners were dying on them." These "humanitarian reasons," though, will also involve—as he goes on to admit—the repeated brutalization of the women. Paulina's experience of not being saved
is thus also bound up with the very perpetuation of her life. And it is this
betrayal into life that is itself, intricately associated with—and symbolized
by—the betrayal in the use of the music. As Paulina's life becomes part of
Roberto's "game," so is her listening betrayed by its very survival: the capacity to hear now becomes the site of a reenactment of the torture. Thus
losing the capacity to *listen* on her own terms, Paulina loses listening as a
possible form of singular testimony, as a way in which she might remember
and tell others of what has happened and thus be able to bear witness to her
disappearing past.

Paulina's active hearing has thus been "played" like an instrument and is
inscribed in a scene from which it cannot remove itself as a listener and
hence not become an active site of testimony.[36] Her inscription in Roberto's
performance—too soon for her to realize, too late for her later to undo—
returns in her later life as a constant reenactment of what she can no longer
simply hear or tell. The past thus disappears in this *betrayal of listening*, a
betrayal that appears, on the level of the play itself, to infect all forms of
hearing.[37] The torture disappears itself in the very act of listening, and returns later only to disappear, *to disappear its evidence* once again.

A GHOSTLY ARCHIVE

The importance of listening as the site of evidence—not only as *the tool for
perceiving evidence* but as *a form of evidence itself*—is emphasized in this
scene by the use of the tape recorder, both for Paulina, who provides a
staged testimony for a "Commission," and Roberto, who provides a staged
testimony for a "trial." Indeed, just as the music in the scene—also presumably played from a cassette player—hovers over the scene from some recorder offstage, so the dictations of Paulina and Roberto also hover from
tape recorders not exactly present in the staging, since we have been told in
the stage directions at the beginning of the play that there is only one tape

recorder on the stage. In this scene the tape recorder thus essentially splits into three and takes on a role of its own, another character that links the problem of listening to the music to the problem of listening to the story of disappearance as a form of evidence.

This split function of the cassette recorder is also explicitly marked by the use of the verb *tocar*, the verb for "performance" that comes to mean something new in relation to this machine. Early in the play, after making Roberto listen to the tape of Schubert, Paulina turns to another activity, the recording of Roberto's words on the tape recorder, hoping to force him to confess:

> Paulina: You should know, Doctor, that everything you say will be recorded here.
>
> . . . .
>
> *Brief pause. Paulina switches on the recorder.*
>
> . . . .
>
> Roberto: Escobar. This is inexcusable. I will never forgive you as long as I live.
> Paulina: Hold on, hold on. Stop right there, Doctor. Let's see if this thing is working.
> *She presses some buttons [Toca unos botones] and then we hear Roberto's voice.*
> Roberto's voice from the cassette: Escobar. This is inexcusable. I will never forgive you as long as I live.
> Paulina's voice from the cassette: Hold on, hold on. Stop right there, Doctor. Let's see.
> *Paula stops the recorder.*
> Paulina: Ready. It's recording everything marvelously. . . .
>
> . . . .
>
> *She presses another button [Toca otro botón].* (DM, 31–32; MD, 43–45)

The first scene of recording, here, is a scene of repetition: of Roberto's and Paulina's words played back immediately after they are spoken, which as such repeat, though in a somewhat different manner, the other various forms of verbal repetition throughout the play.[38] While the replaying of Roberto's words is explicitly meant as a testing of the capacity to record and archive Roberto's confession, to use it as permanent evidence that Paulina may keep as proof of what happened to her,[39] the performance of switching on and off the machine, highlighted by the stage directions, also points to the production of this recording as a scene of power and control: of turning on the recorder, but also of turning it off. The verb *tocar*, here, translated as "press," emphasizes the force involved in the act of recording, a force that may be used to make possible, or to interrupt, a testimony. The act of archiving is thus played out as a performing that is a pressing, a pushing of buttons that may make speaking, and listening, equally begin and cease.

The double-sided nature of the force involved in recording, performed first in terms of the stopping and starting of the machine, may be said to extend, as well, to the inscription process of the recording on the tape, a function that is hinted at in the word that names the tape cassette player most often in the play, *grabadora* (appearing twenty-four times in the Spanish version of the play). The word *grabadora* is linked etymologically to the word for "engrave" (*grabar*), and thus, like the word for writing, *scribere*, gestures back to a meaning that involves a violent cutting rather than a simple form of mirroring or representation.[40] The tape, becoming with the recorder a kind of automatic ear,[41] is inscribed upon by the sound, and thus, even at the moment that it is controlled by Paulina, seems to figure (or repeat) the manner in which *she* was inscribed by the event of her forced listening to the music and words of Roberto. Attempting to control the recorder and to tape Roberto's voice and words in order to produce a permanent archive of her torture, Paulina's voice also returns on the tape, alongside Roberto's—not only as the one controlling the recording but also as the one being recorded, being forcibly inscribed on the tape, just as the music coming out of the tape was originally inscribed upon her.[42] In this sense the recorder also serves as the site of the life, and listening, that was not "being saved" but in a certain sense being turned, itself, into a living death, a *grabadora* that is both engraving and grave, the living on of a voice that is also a constant disappearing of the living Paulina, the lingering, in her voice and ear, of her disappearing.[43]

Playing the tape, first as the source of music and then as a means of recording, Paulina presumably attempts to turn the passivity of her violated listening—her violated ear—into a form of activity that will archive the actions of Roberto in a manner that will no longer be erasable, a performance that must be heard. But even as she explains to Gerardo what she hopes to obtain from her actions, she supplements the recording with two other forms of archival activity: "I want him to confess," Paulina tells Gerardo early on in the play. "I want him to sit in front of that cassette recorder and tell me what he did—and then have him write it out in his own handwriting and sign it and I would keep a copy forever" (*DM*, 41). Indeed, at the end of her interaction with Roberto, toward the end of the play, Paulina remains unsatisfied with Roberto's recorded "confession." After listening to it, Paulina still feels that justice has not been done, and after Robert claims that the confession was false, she threatens, again, to kill him:

Roberto: What more do you want? . . .
Paulina: The truth, Doctor. The truth and I'll let you go. Repent and I'll let you go. You have ten seconds. . . . (DM, 65)[44]

At the end of the scene, we see Roberto and Paulina suspended in this position, leaving the audience in uncertainty over whether or not Paulina has killed Roberto. The suspension of Paulina between hearing and performing, life and death, seems now to take over the audience as well in a final theatrical impasse that repeats the impossibility of producing a mode of performance that can be heard, and listened to, and a form of justice adequate to this story in the aftermath of this disappearing history.

TOUCH WITHOUT TOUCH

If the English version, however, leaves the audience, at this point, in suspension—a suspension that is then extended through the brief closing act of the play—the Spanish version includes a few more lines in Paulina's exchange with Roberto, lines that include another story of performance and of justice:

Roberto: What more do you want? . . .
Paulina: The truth, Doctor. The truth and I'll let you go. You will be as free as Cain when he killed his brother and he repented. God put a mark on him so that no one could touch him. (MD, 81, my translation)

The story of Cain and Abel is a "primeval" story of punishment, as the scholar Claus Westermann notes—a story that occurs as a kind of foundation, rather than one that, as we might elaborate, occurs within the terms of an already established law.[45] Paulina seems to be searching, here, for a mode of justice, then, that could establish justice for her in different terms from the ones she is given by Gerardo's human rights commission, and outside the impasse between law and revenge. While Paulina notably suggests a form of punishment that would preserve Roberto's life, the preservation she suggests is also a form of punishment in itself: the punishment of a wandering, like Cain, away from the presence of society, a kind of survival that is also an absolute loss. In this sense, the punishment would resemble the experience of Paulina herself, who is preserved from being murdered but only in order to suffer more.

Yet Paulina's particular phrasing of the biblical line that describes God's protection of Cain clearly distinguishes the punishment of Cain from Paulina's own torture, and makes this distinction by precisely substituting, in the line concerning God's protection of Cain, another word for the usual "attack" or "murder" (*atavar* or *matar*, usually used to translate the Hebrew verb), the word translated here as "touch"—yet another meaning of the verb *tocar*: "God put a mark on him so that no one could touch him [*que nadie lo pudiera tocar*]." Describing a marking that preserves Cain from being touched, Paulina imagines a mode of action that would both punish and archive the crime through the removal of touch, by creating an existence, that is, devoid of touch. What Paulina offers potentially to Roberto is, then, neither a death sentence nor a pardon, but rather a punishment that banishes without erasing, that archives the crime through the mark, even as it banishes the criminal from society's presence. Paulina, herself punished by the violent touch of Roberto and his music—and consequently unable, we are implicitly told, to feel the touch of her husband or her music[46]—wishes not so much to kill or to pardon as to mark, to bring back into history the act by which her own and others' ability to listen, to know the crime, has been disappeared, so as to reclaim the possibility of her capacity to listen, to perform the act of listening that will teach others to listen to—to be touched as well by—her story.[47] And as such not only to refer to, to understand, but also to pass on, *in the performance of the very act of listening*, the evidence of an event that can no longer be reduced to the simple referent of any language.

MOVING SOUNDS

What kind of performance would mark, or touch, without touch? As the last dialogue between Paulina and Roberto ends, we are told by the stage directions that they "are covered from view by a giant mirror that descends, forcing the members of the audience to look at themselves" (*DM*, 66). In this scene, the audience is brought onto the stage as part of the performance and reenactment that threatens to engulf the entire viewing—and listening—of the play. In this strange staging of this mirror, as well, in a "phantasmagoric" light,[48] we discover that Paulina once again sees Roberto, neither certainly alive nor dead. The play maintains the action of performance—focused on seeing and looking—in a kind of suspension, between living and dead, and between appearing and disappearing.

But these actions and ghostly sightings take place, as well, to the sound of the Schubert quartet, which begins to be heard from somewhere offstage. What we hear, then, is the very music that was played while Paulina was tortured, and which she played, herself, while interrogating Roberto. Now, however, Paulina sits and listens to the music with her husband:

> *Gerardo and Paulina sit in their seats. Roberto goes to another seat, always looking at Paulina. Applause is heard when the imaginary musicians come on. The instruments are tested and tuned. Then* Death and the Maiden *begins. Gerardo looks at Paulina, who looks forward. After a few instants, she turns slowly and looks at Roberto. Their eyes interlock for a moment. Then she turns her head and faces the stage and the mirror. The lights go down while the music plays and plays and plays.* (DM, 68)

In the final lines, Paulina turns away from Roberto while the music plays and plays and plays [*mientras la música toca y toca y toca*]. The verb *tocar* reappears here, repeated three times at the very end of the play in its written stage directions, now signifying "playing" or "performing," not in the theatrical sense but rather in the explicitly musical sense. What kind of touch, and what kind of action or performance is this? Is Paulina touched, moved— two other meanings of *tocar*—by this music, the touching of the strings that makes the moving sound? Does her turning to and away from Roberto figure her inability, or her ability, to be touched by this particular performance? What can be heard in the sound of this music and in the playing of this quartet?

DEATH AND THE MAIDEN

Earlier in the play, Roberto, playing for his life as he asked for pardon in front of the cassette recorder, was involved in a set of recordings that copied voice in a seemingly endless process of distanced and undone presence or truth: from his live voice, to the tape recorder, to the transcription from the tape recorder, back to his voice reading the transcription, and then to a signature that, later, he will claim to be merely staged, a false confession.[49] The suspension between the live and nonlive voice in the cassette recorder left the characters hovering in the ghostly world of their disappearance.

The music of Schubert, however, that is performed at the end (or is played back on a tape as if performed) begins in the opposite direction: from a notational script that, never live, begins anew only when it achieves sound through the instrument.[50] In this particular quartet by Schubert, moreover, the music—the notation, the marks of sound—itself repeats and translates the notes of a song by Schubert, the song "Death and the Maiden," which, itself, was Schubert's musical translation of a poem by Matthias Claudius. The music, then, is a series of marks or notations that repeat and change each other, that touch and don't touch as they set the conditions of the performance of a song that passes into the sound of a quartet, not quite appearing there but also not quite disappearing, a touching, moving song whose force continues into its musical afterlives or survivals.

"Death and the Maiden" is a song, moreover, *about* touching and not touching, a dialogue between a young woman and death. The first stanza is spoken by the woman:

> Vorüber! Ach Vorüber!
> Geh, wilder Knochenman!
> Ich ben noch jung! Geh lieber,
> Und rühre mich nicht an.
> Und rühre mich nicht an.

> Pass me by! Oh, pass me by!
> Go, fierce man of bones!
> I am still young! Go rather,
> And do not touch me.
> And do not touch me.

The words "do not touch me [*rühre mich nicht an*]"—which would be translated into Spanish as *no me tocque*—are a plea by the woman not to be touched by death. But what does it mean to be touched by death? Already, the possibility of touching occurs, in this poem, by means of a figure, the figure by which the woman addresses Death as a character, someone who can (and does in the poem) respond to her address. Here, in this poem, voice is a figure not only of death but also of the maiden, whom Death addresses in his turn, and in so doing has already begun to bring into his world. The voice of the song that performs the notes to this poem, I would suggest, and the sound of the quartet that performs the notes of the song, carry, unconsciously, the figure of the maiden's voice, and the German words, passed on, in the play, through the Spanish, both touching and not touching death, both touched and not touched by it. The plea returns, that is, not as a disappearing, but rather as the marking of a touch, Cain's mark, perhaps, touching us on the head so that we may live on, moved by the music or moved to repeat it in a new way.

Do we hear, in this music, the voice of the young woman, or the repetitive, single note of death?[51] In the repetitions of this performance, this thrice-repeated performance of the music that "plays and plays and plays [*toca y toca y toca*]" is perhaps the model of an act that may make a difference—the difference between performing and performing and performing (or touching and touching and touching, *toca y toca y toca*), between German and Spanish, Spanish and English—by passing on, without touch, the touch of those who have disappeared and returned.

CHAPTER FIVE

Psychoanalysis in the Ashes of History

Wilhelm Jensen, Sigmund Freud, and Jacques Derrida

> Memories of her village peopled by the dead
> turned slowly to ash and in their place a single
> image arose. Fire.
>
> TONI MORRISON, *A Mercy*

IN AN ESSAY OF 1907, "Delusion and Dream in Wilhelm Jensen's *Gradiva*," Sigmund Freud analyzes the novella *Gradiva: A Pompeiian Fantasy* as a story exemplifying the principles of psychoanalysis laid out in *The Interpretation of Dreams*.[1] In Jensen's story, a young archaeologist becomes obsessed with the figure of a walking woman on a bas-relief he has seen on a trip to Italy. He names her "Gradiva" and, convinced by a dream that the woman had died in Pompeii during the eruption of Vesuvius in AD 79, he travels to the ruined city in order to search for the singular traces of her toe-prints in the ash.

In this archaeological love story set amid the ruins of Pompeii, Freud finds an allegory for repression and the reemergence of repressed desire. In a later reading of Freud's text, the twentieth-century philosopher Jacques Derrida, in his book *Archive Fever* (*Mal d'Archive*),[2] discovers, inside Freud's figure of the archaeological dig, what Derrida calls an "archival" drive, a pain, and a suffering (*mal*) that bears witness to the suffering, and evil, of a unique twentieth-century history. Derrida proposes that the history of the twentieth century can best be thought through its relation to the "archive," a psychic as well as technical procedure of recording or of "writing" history that participates not only in its remembering but also in its forgetting.

At the heart of psychoanalysis, Derrida suggests, is the thinking of an archival drive that simultaneously yearns after memory and offers the potential for its radical elimination. Beginning from a reflection on the main argument of *Archive Fever* concerning the nature of the psychoanalytic archive, I will argue that the texts of Freud and Derrida, read together, ultimately enable a rethinking of the very nature of history around the possibility of its erasure. Moving beyond what Derrida explicitly suggests, I will also argue that these insights about history can ultimately be understood only from within the literary story of Norbert Hanold, the archaeologist, and in particular the story of his dream. In what follows I will begin with Derrida's general reflections on the archive and ultimately turn to the story of the dream, which is perhaps also that of psychoanalytic dreaming more generally, to ask: What does it mean for history to be a history of ashes? And how does psychoanalysis bear witness to such a history?

I

A BURNING ARCHIVE

The problem of the archive as an immediate contemporary question of historical memory first emerges in *Archive Fever* in the opening "Insert" ("Prière d'insérer") where Derrida links the archive to the urgency of twentieth-century history:

> Why reelaborate today a *concept of the archive*? In a single configuration, equally technical and political, ethical and juridical?
>
> This essay will designate the horizon of this question discreetly, so burning is its evidence. The disasters that mark this end of the millennium are also *archives of evil*: dissimulated or destroyed, prohibited, diverted, "repressed." Their treatment is equally massive and refined in the course of civil or international wars, of private or secret manipulations. No one ever renounces—and this is the unconscious itself—the appropriation of power over the document, over its detention, retention, or its interpretation.[3]

The question of the archive is a question of "today"—of a particular historical period, a question with its own historical place—because it is linked, today, to the "disasters that mark the end of the millennium." These disasters are not simply the objects of archives, or objects that call out for archiving; they are also, themselves, unique events whose archives have been repressed or erased, and whose singularity, as events, can be defined by that erasure. They can indeed themselves be called "*archives du mal*"—archives of evil (or suffering)—because they not only leave an impression but hide their impression. They involve evil or suffering, that is, precisely because they hide or prohibit their own memory: because they are themselves "hidden or destroyed, prohibited, diverted, repressed." They consist precisely in hiding themselves; they become events insofar as they are, precisely, hidden.

The thinking of the archive is, in this sense, not only a thinking of memory but a thinking of history, and one that marks in particular, as I will argue, the historicity of the twentieth, and now twenty-first, centuries. This history is not, as one might traditionally expect, constituted by events that create their own remembrance, but by events that destroy their own remembrance. "Think of the debates around all the 'revisionisms,'" says Derrida, "and think of the seismic movements of historiography, of the technological upheavals in the constitution and treatment of so many 'dossiers'" (PI, 2). This is why, I would suggest, psychoanalysis must be brought together with the thinking of the archive, because psychoanalysis has long been interested in the relation between history—personal and collective history—and the ways that its memory is suppressed or repressed: the ways that history is not available for immediate conscious access. Indeed, psychoanalysis must itself be understood, Derrida argues, primarily *as* an archival science. Psychoanalysis, I would suggest, can thus help us to think, and perhaps witness, a new kind of event that is constituted, paradoxically, by the way it disappears.

RETURN AND REPETITION

The archival figure emerges from, and also reinterprets, Freud's own famous figure for psychoanalytic discovery, the metaphor of the archaeological dig.[4] From 1896 onward Freud had repeatedly represented the surprising encounter with the unconscious through an analogy in which the unconscious aspects of the mind are likened to a buried city that occasionally shows signs of its presence and eventually comes to light in analysis. But at the heart of the archaeological metaphor, Derrida notes, we often find a different kind of figure, not the figure of buried objects but rather of buried writing:

> [Psychoanalysis] does not, by accident, privilege the figures of the imprint and of imprinting. Installing itself often in the scene of the archaeological dig, its discourse concerns, first of all, the stock of "impressions" and the deciphering of inscriptions, but also their censorship and repression, the repression and the reading of registrations. (PI, 2)

If the archaeological project is the uncovering of an object, the archival task is the reading of an inscription. In this reading, psychoanalytic discourse does not only unveil a meaning of "impressions" and their "repression" but also "installs *itself*" at the heart of the dig. The psychoanalyst's act of interpretation does not, therefore, simply reveal what has been repressed, but may also repress again what has been inscribed. "Is it not necessary," Derrida asks, "to begin by distinguishing the archive from that to which it is too often reduced, notably the experience of *memory* and the return to the *origin*, but also the *archaic* and the *archeological*, the memory or the dig, in short, the search for lost time?" (PI, 1–2).

Psychoanalysis does not permit a simple "return to the origin" because the impression it reads is not only left *for* psychoanalysis but also left *on* psychoanalysis as it encounters the surprise of the inscription, and ultimately *by* psychoanalysis as it deciphers, as it leaves its own impressions, right at the site of the original ones, in a new archival act. The encounter with the archive is thus an act of interpretation that appears like a return, but it is also an event that partially represses, as it passes on, the inscriptions it encounters; that passes on not only an impression but also, somewhat differently, its repression. The deciphering of desire, at the scene of the dig, is thus also the communication, and repression, of desire, not necessarily of erotic desire, but rather of archival desire, "this fever, this presence, this desire [of Freud]," as Jacques Lacan described it.[5] Through the act of its own archival drive, in other words, psychoanalysis reveals an "absolute desire for memory" (PI, 3)—its own desire and perhaps *also* a desire at the heart of the erotic—that attempts to return to the past but to some extent always repeats and passes on, in its very act of interpretation, the ways in which the past has been erased.

As a thinking of the archive, psychoanalysis thus becomes witness to the strange notion of a *memory* that *erases*, a new notion of memory that, I would argue, is at the heart of the notion of "archive fever" (*mal d'archive*). Indeed, I would suggest, Derrida's description of the archive in psychoanalytic thought alludes to a very specific and historically situated archival discovery, Freud's encounter with "repetition compulsion" after World War I and his reformulation of the content and form of psychoanalytic theory around the notion of the "death drive," another term that "archive fever" arguably attempts to translate. Freud, as we recall, described, in *Beyond the Pleasure Principle*, his encounter with a kind of memory of events that erased, rather than produced, conscious recall: the dreams and memories of the soldiers of World War I whose death encounters repeatedly returned to interrupt, rather than enter, consciousness. No longer capable of interpreting these memories as expressions of unconscious desire, Freud came to understand them as repetitions of the experiences that the soldiers could not grasp, a form of memory that, in enacting what it could not recall, also passed on a historical event that this memory erased. These memories, in other words, in repeating and erasing, did not *represent* but rather *enacted* history; they *made* history by also erasing it. They were, themselves, archival memories because they archived history by effacing it; and in effacing history, they also created it. The solders became, as it were, self-erasing inscriptions of history. Traumatic memory thus totters between remembrance and erasure, producing a history that is, in its very events, a kind of inscription of the past; but also a history constituted by the erasure of its traces.

Psychoanalysis can thus think the singularity of twentieth-century history, the new impression it makes, because, as an archival theory, it describes the way memory can *make* history precisely by *erasing* it. The notion of the archive, as I would thus interpret both Freud and Derrida, is a *change in modes of memory* that is also a *change in history*, a change that is "equally technological and political, ethical and juridical" (PI, 1). It is this surprising change in memory and history, moreover, that is reflected in Freud's reconfiguration of the notion of the drive as a death drive. Although it is called a "drive," it is *also* a *new* discovery in history—a new shift in the nature of the historical archive—whose own past cannot be traced, because it is effaced, and is thus named only in terms of the way it erases the archive of memory, including the archive of its own memory:

> This drive . . . always operates in silence, it never leaves an archive of its own. (*AF*, 10)

> [I]t's silent vocation is to burn the archive and to incite amnesia. (*AF*, 12)

> [E]nlisting the in-finite, archive fever touches on radical evil. (*AF*, 19–20)

Between the shock of the memory that effaces, and the shock of the discovery of this memory, is the event of an erasure, and of a history, that carries the name of the death drive, which is also archive fever, because it is made up of memory and is about memory, it is about the burning desire for memory and the history of its burning up.

II

FREUD'S FEVER

How can psychoanalysis bear witness to this erasure, beyond repression, which is new to the twentieth century? We should note that the concept of archive fever, and its fundamental psychoanalytic ancestors, the notions of traumatic repetition and of the death drive, themselves, as concepts, enact a kind of return and repetition, a memory and its erasure. Indeed, *Beyond the Pleasure Principle*, in its attempt to provide an economic understanding of the mind and in particular in its return to the notion of the memory trace, brings us back to Freud's first full attempt at a psychic system, the 1895 *Project for a Scientific Psychology*. It is on the level of the formation of psychoanalytic concepts, then, in the way that Freud's concepts inscribe a memory, archive their own history within themselves, that psychoanalytic discourse will bear witness to the history that psychoanalysis encounters. The notion of the history *referred to* by the concept of "archive" is available only by studying the *history of the concept* of the archive, a story that occurs not on the level of a simple narration but, itself, requires a new temporal and historical modality.

What we find, indeed, when we return from *Beyond the Pleasure Principle* to its apparent origins in *The Project for a Scientific Psychology* is a concept of memory as inscription and repetition that cannot be located simply in the past of Freud's work. For the concept of the memory trace in the *Project* itself describes a form of memory that has no simple beginning, and which is a meeting between forces that is also a breaching and inscription, the marking of a path, and the deferral of quantity.[6] Memory thus originates as its own deferral and also as its later repetition, a fundamental *deferral and repetition at the beginning*. The notion of the memory trace, in other words, "at the beginning" of Freud's itinerary, already anticipates the concept of repetition compulsion. Returning to the beginning, then, the concepts of *Beyond the Pleasure Principle* repeat, and erase, this past, erase it to the extent that *Nachträglichkeit* (deferred action) no longer operates as a term within this later text, precisely at the moment that repetition and delay nonetheless dominate its notion of human history.[7]

Indeed, the concept of *Nachträglichkeit* is the central concept, I would argue, that Derrida attempts to rename in the concept of the archive. This psychoanalytic concept of deferred action enacts its own deferred action and its own repetition throughout Freud's career, but in doing so it also both records and effaces its own past, and to a certain extent becomes erased from the psychoanalytic archive. We see this self-archiving and self-erasing act in *Beyond the Pleasure Principle*, where the notion of a deferred experience is newly figured as an "attempt to return" by consciousness that ultimately fails and departs into the repetitions of a future history. Trauma, and ultimately life and the drive itself, is an attempt to return that instead departs. This figure, this concept, this story—the story also, we recall, of the child who plays "*fort/da*" with his spool—is about memory and history, and it is also the concept archiving its own history, as it returns, and departs, from its origins.[8]

The psychoanalytic concept, I am trying to suggest, archives its own history and in so doing bears witness to the newness, and alterity, to the shock of a history it cannot assimilate but only repeat. The twentieth-century history to which psychoanalysis bears witness through its own historical unfolding is the intersection of these two dimensions—of the concept that repeats, and of the memory that erases. Which is also to say that what Freud shows us, in the peculiar unfolding of his own discourse, is that the history of World War I can be understood, precisely, as a history constituted by the erasure of its own memory.

DISAPPEARING HISTORY

In the structure and history of its concepts, psychoanalysis thus registers the impact of a new self-erasing history. To cite Robert Jay Lifton, psychoanalysis is, itself, a "survivor" of World War I.[9] But this survival, which gives psychoanalysis, we might say, its own "survivor mission," its mission to witness not only the individual but also collective history—a collective history that is beginning to disappear even as it is being produced—is also structured by the principle of *Nachträglichkeit*, by the passage into the future that constitutes all traumatic experience. Indeed, the concept of return and departure, so central to *Beyond the Pleasure Principle*, will repeat itself, in *Moses and Monotheism*, now as the story of Moses attempting to return the Hebrews to Canaan. The Hebrews murder him, and depart, traumatically, into the future of Jewish monotheistic history.

At the center of *Archive Fever*, this story—which Derrida addresses through an encounter with the book *Freud's Moses: Psychoanalysis Terminable and Interminable* by the Jewish historian Yosef Hayim Yerushalmi[10]—will return, once again, as a story *about psychoanalysis*. What brings Derrida to Yerushalmi's book is the question of whether or not psychoanalysis is a Jewish science, a question that, for Yerushalmi, means that it is a science of, and always opening up to, the future. But the return and departure that constitutes the survival of the Jews in *Moses and Monotheism*, read as a traumatic (archival) history, is also the story, I would argue, of psychoanalytic thought, which ultimately conceives both the erasure of the history it witnesses and, potentially, the erasure of its own history, that is, the very history of psychoanalysis *as witness*. This is why, I believe, Derrida ultimately turns to this work, and to Yerushalmi's book, to talk about the question of futurity that lies not only at the heart of all trauma—as deferral and future repetition, as an attempted return that instead departs—but also lies specifically at the heart of the archival history of psychoanalysis at this moment of its conceptualization, in Vienna in the late thirties. If psychoanalysis, in its thinking of *Nachträglichkeit*, witnesses a history that is constituted by the erasure of memory, then Freud also, I would suggest, in *Moses and Monotheism*, conceives—or narrates—the possibility of a history constituted *by the erasure of its own witness*, a history that burns away the very possibility of *conceiving* memory, that leaves the future itself, in ashes.

III

PSYCHOANALYSIS IN THE ASHES

Yet at this very point in *Archive Fever*, in the ashes of history, at its site, another story is told, the story of the German writer Wilhelm Jensen's *Gradiva: A Pompeiian Fantasy* and of Freud's reading of his novella in "Delusion and Dream in Wilhelm Jensen's *Gradiva*." We turn back, in Derrida's "Postscript," to this earlier Freud text, written in 1907 after *The Interpretation of Dreams*, to discover an encounter between Freud and a dream, or rather, between Freud and a literary text about dreams that returns us to the site of a disaster, and to the site of literature, *to the site of literature as archive*.

To recapitulate the story briefly, it is, as you will remember, the story of a young German archaeologist, Norbert Hanold, who becomes obsessed with the plaster cast of a marble Roman copy of a Greek bas-relief he has found in Italy and managed to purchase upon his return to Germany. Enthralled by the position of one of her feet, he names her "Gradiva" ("she who walks") and, having become convinced, in his fantasies, that she was from Pompeii, he decides, after a dream, that she was buried there during the eruption of AD 79. He ultimately returns to Pompeii to search for her traces in the ash, and, encountering a woman he believes is Gradiva's specter, engages in a series of conversations with her that finally bring him to the realization that she is in fact his old neighbor Zoe Bertgang, for whom his desire is now, finally and consciously, aroused.[11]

Freud, who had traveled to Naples in 1902, thinks of Gradiva, when he thinks of his new science, after encountering in the story, by surprise, his own discovery:

> There is . . . no better analogy for repression, by which something in the mind is at once made inaccessible and preserved, than burial of the sort to which Pompeii fell a victim and from which it could emerge once more through the work of spades. Thus it was that the young archaeologist was obliged in his phantasy to transport to Pompeii the original of the relief which reminded him of the object of his forgotten youthful love. The author was well justified, indeed, in lingering over the valuable similarity which his delicate sense had traced out between a piece of mental action in the individual and an isolated historical process in the history of mankind.[12]

The analogy of burial and preservation, by which Freud had in 1896 characterized his own discovery of the unconscious, is rediscovered here in a literary text in a peculiarly self-reflexive way: first of all, as a figure used unconsciously and symptomatically by the main character, the archaeologist Norbert Hanold, a figure that represents his own unconscious processes. And second, as a figure used by the author of the story, who "traces out" the similarity between the burial of Pompeii and the "process of the mind." Character and author are thus both tracers of footprints in the ash of a catastrophe; they "linger" [*verweilen*] at this moment of discovery, a pleasurable erotic lingering and perhaps also one tinged with a Faustian threat.[13] Freud too, we could say, as a lover—not of a woman but of a science—confronted by Jensen's text, is "reminded" of "the forgotten object of his youthful love," psychoanalysis, or a "piece" of psychoanalysis, a piece of its "historical" if not material truth, which, "by analogy," he must not only make emerge once more "through the work of spades" (that is, dig up, with pleasure, as an archaeologist) but must also trace out, pursue with fright, *in the ashes.*

Freud's encounter with this text, therefore, does not involve an act of recognition, but rather a repetition that burns with a passion for discovery, *beyond* that of the character Norbert Hanold. Yet Hanold, himself is, already, no longer an archaeologist, but rather an archivist. "Hanold suffers from archive fever," Derrida writes, "he has exhausted the science of archaeology. . . . This science itself was of the past." Hanold returns to Pompeii not in order to return to life—the life of Gradiva, and ultimately the life of "Zoe"—but rather to find Gradiva's singular "traces," something he comes to understand, in the story, at a moment of memory. At this moment in the story, Hanold stands alone in the silent streets of Pompeii, which suddenly seems peopled by the dead (as Derrida summarizes Jensen):

> Hanold understands everything. He understands why he had traveled through Rome and Naples. He begins to *know* (*wissen*) what he did not then know, namely his "intimate drive" or "impulse." And this knowledge, this comprehension, this deciphering of the interior desire to decipher which drove him on to Pompeii, all of this comes back to him in an act of memory (*Erinnerung*). He recalls that he came to see if he could find her traces, the traces of Gradiva's footsteps. (*AF*, 98)

Hanold does not wish to see Gradiva, but to revisit what makes her memory possible: the traces of her steps. Remembering traces, he thus, I would suggest, also understands (or theorizes), belatedly; like the Freud of both the *Project* and *Beyond the Pleasure Principle*, he attempts to return to the origin of his own memory as the origin of Gradiva's traces. As I would interpret this moment, staged by the philosopher as a moment of conceptualization—of theorization that echoes Freud's own belated creation of psychoanalytic theory—Hanold thus wishes to return to the *possibility* of Gradiva's memory, to what will guarantee that she is memorable *in the future*. That she can no longer be forgotten, erased, excised from the archive, that her impression will remain, and her history will intertwine itself with his.

In Freud's own act of encounter with Hanold's trace, I would also argue, in repeating Hanold's gesture, he feverishly repeats or "outbids" Hanold, for he too attempts to return, but he does so in Hanold's (and his own) future: he attempts to return to the possibility of another memory, that of his own love of his youth, psychoanalysis, as the very possibility of testimony. Derrida writes of the moment, in Jensen's story, of feverish conceptualization: "He dreams this irreplaceable place, the very ash, where the singular imprint, like a signature, barely distinguishes itself from the impression. And this is the condition of singularity, the idiom, the secret, testimony" (*AF*, 99). Hanold's dreaming, and Freud's after him, I believe, raise urgent questions, questions beyond their concepts, beyond the fever of conceptualization, at this burning site: How can I bear witness, Hanold wonders, how can I guarantee the memory of Gradiva? How can I bear witness, how testify, Freud unconsciously thus asks, to the traces of psychoanalysis, that is, to the very possibility of finding traces, to the very possibility of memory, in the ash of this conceptualization and in the ash of this memory?

BURNING DREAMS

Hanold, at this site, "dreams," "he dreams . . . the very ash." What does it mean to dream? If we look at the larger context of the passage to which Derrida refers above, we notice that the object of Hanold's memory, his reason for coming to Pompeii is, in fact, a dream. Even while Derrida writes that Hanold "dreams," the actual dream of Hanold, to which he alludes, is to a certain extent effaced from the philosopher's text, as the dream is also effaced from many critical texts on Jensen and Freud. It is, then, a dream that repeatedly recedes into unconsciousness, though it is, I would argue, at the very heart of Jensen's story. This is Hanold's first dream of Gradiva, while still in Germany, and the first moment that he actually sees her. I quote the entire context of the passage from Jensen in which Hanold, in Pompeii, comes to remember this dream. It begins as he stands in Pompeii's streets:

> Hanold . . . looked before him down the Strada di Mercurio . . .
> Then suddenly—
> With open eyes he gazed along the street, yet it seemed to him as if he were doing it in a dream. A little to the right something suddenly stepped forth . . . and across the lava stepping-stones, which led from the house to the other side of the Strada di Mercurio, Gradiva stepped buoyantly.

. . . .

As soon as he caught sight of her, Norbert's memory was clearly awakened
to the fact that he had seen her here once already in a dream, walking thus,
the night that she had lain down as if to sleep. . . . With this memory he
became conscious, for the first time, of something else; he had, without
himself knowing the motive in his heart . . . come to Pompeii to see if he
could here find trace of her. (G, 48–50)

Hanold's act of remembering the reason for his trip to Pompeii is part of a
complex scene of dreaming and awakening. Hanold's remembering, his moment of conceptualization, is a belated awakening to the fact that his seeing
of her is a repetition, the repetition of a previous dream, which appears after
the fact, that is, to be a dream of following traces.

This "frightful" dream, indeed, appears to constitute the figurative center
of the story, and thus a kind of originary moment of Norbert's history. The
dream in fact constitutes Norbert's first sighting of Gradiva, as well as the
place in which he also first sees the destruction of Pompeii:

In it he was in old Pompeii, and on the twenty-fourth of August of the year
79, which witnessed the eruption of Vesuvius. The heavens held the doomed
city wrapped in a black mantle of smoke. . . . [T]he pebbles and the rain of
ashes fell down on Norbert also. . . . As he stood thus . . . he suddenly saw
Gradiva a short distance in front of him. . . . Violent fright forced from him a
cry of warning. She heard it, too, for her head turned toward him so that her
face now appeared for a moment in full view. . . . At the same time, her face
became paler as if it were changing to white marble. . . . [H]astening quickly
after her . . . he found his way to the place where she had disappeared from
his view, and there she lay . . . as if for sleep, but no longer breathing. . . .
[H]er features quickly became more indistinct as the wind drove to the place
the rain of ashes. . . .

When Norbert Hanold awoke, he still heard the confused cries of the
Pompeiians who were seeking safety. . . . (G, 11–14, translation modified)

Confronted with this "frightfully anxiety-producing dream," Freud suggests
that it is an anxiety dream illustrative of his dream theory. The anxiety of
the dream and the destruction of Pompeii illustrate the repressed and returning erotic desire for Norbert's long-forgotten neighbor Zoe. Freud thus reads
the dream through the archaeological metaphor, as both the burying and
partial reappearance of desire, a wish-fulfillment.

Yet Freud's interpretation has an uncanny effect: for the dream is thus
not only *read* archaeologically but also becomes thereby a *staging* of its own

formation, a staging of the burial of Pompeii, which is the figure of repression. It is a dream of the origin of dreaming, of the possibility of knowing and not knowing, of figuring without consciousness, a mode of witnessing that originates in a catastrophe.

What kind of origin is this dream? Freud himself, at the end of his essay, famously adds an odd afterthought about another motive for the dream:

> This was the wish, comprehensible to every archaeologist, to have been an eye-witness of that catastrophe of 79. What sacrifice would be too great, for an antiquarian, to realize this wish otherwise than through dreams! (255)

The wish to be an eyewitness of catastrophe is Freud's wish, here expressed on the level of manifest content in the dream. But Freud also, I would suggest, sees, and doesn't see, something in the witnessing that the dream narrates, an origin and a catastrophe that is not exactly a burial, and not simply of the past. Indeed, the figure of the destruction of Pompeii is not precisely, or not simply, a figure of burial, since the peculiarity of this "singular historical event" is that the destruction occurred not only through burial but through burial *by ashes*, which is also a burning up, a destruction that does not simply preserve but may also totally incinerate the bodies it buries.[14] At the origin of the figure of repression is the possibility of a complete erasure, which the archaeological analogy of burial and preservation—and the concept of repression that it shapes—itself erases and bypasses, passes over to pass on.

As a narrative, the story of the dream tells not only of a burial, indeed, but of Gradiva's walking, "stepping," and of Norbert Hanold's following of her steps. Step after step, the dream narrates a tracing of steps, which Hanold will remember, later, when his memory is "awoken," as the attempt to find the singular "traces" of her "toe-prints" in the ash.[15] The tracing is both Norbert Hanold's, then, and also "the author's," who had linked the "singular" destruction of Pompeii to the process of the mind, which is also Freud's "fine sense," as a theoretician whose concepts must also be figures, and often literary figures. What Freud sees and doesn't see in this dream, what he attempts to return to but must repeat and erase, I would suggest, is the origin of his own theory, his own theory of dreams, not only in *The Interpretation of Dreams* but in the memory traces of the *Project*. These traces of the past—the past of Freud's own theory—are also traces of the future, insofar as the dream, a dream of burning that is also an awakening, points us toward the other kind of nightmares, the *nightmares that awaken*, which are the traumatic dreams of *Beyond the Pleasure Principle*.

In these ashes, the figure that dominates is rather, as I see it, the figure of the trace, or even more the action of tracing, the step after step. These steps are dispersed throughout the story both in the dreams or thoughts of Norbert and on the level of the letter: in the *VorGANG* (mental process) that is also an *UnterGANG* (destruction) figured as the creation, and erasure, of the steps of Gradiva, who is also Zoe *BertGANG*, whose steps Norbert follows in the streets of Pompeii, after remembering his dream of ashes. But what, exactly, is the figure of a footstep in the ash? How can ashes sustain a print, when ashes are precisely that which may disperse and drift away? And what would it mean to leave a trace, or a remainder in that which is, itself, a remainder, the ash that is the burned up trace of what is incinerated? The figure of ash is, indeed, not only the substratum *for* a writing that has taken place but the figure *of* a writing that is burning up.

On the site of these ashes, Freud writes a new kind of language. Faced by the dream, he is stirred to seek a saving figure in Zoe (whose name means "life" in Greek), but he gives us in fact another kind of figure, the imagination of an unimaginable erasure that is carried, I would argue, by all of his figures of deferral, of repetition, of return and departure, of *Nachträglichkeit*, of trauma. The language of trauma is the language of this absolute erasure, not imaginable in the past or present but, always, as something missed, and about to return, a possibility, always, of a trauma in the future. This is what it means to say, I would suggest, that the traumatic event *is* its future, is its repetition as something that returns but also returns to erase its past, returns as something other than what one could ever recognize. A singular and new event, but in this case, in Freud's facing of the event in the dream, an event that undoes everything we have thought of as events, as history, because it is a future event that threatens to undo its own future.

In his burning mission, I would ask, does Freud become witness to the ashes that surround him, or endure *as* the remainder that psychoanalysis may also become? Cinders are indeed "incubation of the fire lurking beneath the dust."[16] To burn with archive fever: Does it mean to bear witness, or to be ash?

STRANGE WITNESSES

What, indeed, is the language, or figure, of cinders, which is the language of Freud and of Derrida, if it is "the annihilation of the capacity to bear witness"?[17] What of the readers, for example, who read the figure of ash? We are in truth, Derrida suggests in response to such a question by Elisabeth Weber, "strange witnesses . . . who do not know what they are witnessing. . . . witnesses to something they are not witness to."[18] I would suggest that there is something we could call the language of ashes, which is perhaps a new kind of language that is, for us today, marked historically, at least since the middle of the twentieth century.

Indeed, the figure of ash also refers us to events that may not have a simple referent, but are signs of the unimaginable past or the unimaginable future.[19] A future that, as the psychoanalyst Elaine Caruth once remarked, "hovers as a silence over every psychoanalytic session."[20] Which is why the figure of ashes, though without a simple referent, is without question marked by this twentieth-century historicity, this exposure that is now the condition of our history, and why it is in a literary text—a text that, *itself*, has no single referent, a text that can *figure* what it cannot *think*—that, in both the psychoanalyst's work and in the philosopher's work, these ashes, and this strange witness by Freud and Derrida, first emerge.

We could, from this perspective, translate *Archive Fever* in its "Postscript" into a kind of allegory, installing Derrida's French philosophical language at the heart of Freud's German psychoanalytic archive:

> By chance [*par chance*], I wrote these last words on the rim of Vesuvius, right near Pompeii, less than eight days ago. For more than twenty years, each time I've returned to Naples, I've thought of her [*Gradiva*]. (*AF*, 97)

Derrida's reading of his own burning conceptualization of the archive, born from this reading of Freud and Jensen, thus takes place from a thinking of chance, by a movement within philosophy toward the incalculable:

> Who better than Gradiva, I said to myself this time, the *Gradiva* of Jensen and of Freud, could illustrate . . . this concept of the archive, where it marks in its very structure . . . the formation of every concept, the very history of conception? (*AF*, 97)

The origin of a history, the possibility of conceptualization, of thought—which is also the condition of the possibility of memory, and thus of history—only happens to be thought by chance. It is this singular event of chance from which is born the chance of a writing, and of the writing of a new origination of thought, *after the end*.

But in inscribing his own writing on the rim of Vesuvius and at the heart of Freud's psychoanalytic archive, Derrida also (in part unwittingly) retells his own theoretical work *very like* the story of Hanold, who returns to Pompeii to seek after Gradiva. The philosopher thus writes his theory *inside* the literary story of Norbert Hanold, duplicating Hanold's return to Pompeii, which is where the actual sighting of Gradiva takes place, through his chance meeting of Gradiva, or of that "something" that first passes by his eyes as he stands in the burning streets of Pompeii precisely at midday. The thought of Gradiva is not only Derrida's thought *about* "the *Gradiva* of Jensen and of Freud" but also a Hanold-like thought *of* her. The chance takes place within the literary text and only insofar as Derrida, like Freud, encounters but also misses something crucial that he sees and does not see, the importance of the dream at the very heart of Jensen's story. In this way, Derrida's interpretation not only impresses its own trace upon Freud's and Jensen's texts but is in its turn impressed upon *by* them—impressed into their service, we could say, as the site of witness where chance thoughts and chance words arise. They arise as archive fever, but also as a literary fever beyond and below the concept, beyond and below the feverish attempt at conceptualization.

Indeed, I would suggest that we can read this chance in Derrida's own words about thought and concept (*"la conception même de la conception"*) insofar as they are inscribed in the place of Hanold's story, "right on the ashes" (*à même la cendre*), where "it no longer even makes sense to say 'the very ash' or 'right on the ash' " (*ou il n'y a même plus de sens à dire 'la cendre même' ou 'à même la cendre'*) (*AF*, 97–100, *MdA*, 149–54). In Derrida's French, something repeats—the *même*—the very, the same—but it repeats differently each time, in each different context, by chance.

In order to understand this language, however, we must also recall that Hanold's story, the literary text of Wilhelm Jensen, is itself first told *within a dream*, the dream of Norbert Hanold, which is the dream of returning to Pompeii and seeing Gradiva, by chance, in the ashes. I submit that the philosopher, in turn, can be said to be dreaming throughout the entire work of *Archive Fever*, from its first pages: "I dream now," he says at the beginning of his book, "of having the time to submit for your discussion more than one thesis. . . . This time will never be given to me" (*AF*, 5). Derrida's philosophic and literary dreaming returns, much later in his text, to speak again about time, this time as an argument with the historian Yerushalmi, about the chance that stands between no future and a possible future: "In naming these doors [of the future] . . . I dream of Walter Benjamin [*je rêve à Walter Benjamin*]. In his *Theses on the Philosophy of History*, Benjamin designates the 'narrow door' for the passage of the Messiah, 'at each second' " (*AF*, 69). In dreaming of Walter Benjamin, the German Jewish thinker who died during the Holocaust and who has barely had the time to write, at the beginning of the war, his *Theses* about the philosophy of history and its relation to futurity, Derrida repeats his return to the German language archive as well as to the Jewish thinkers, Freud and Benjamin, in whose writing he finds the chance of a dreaming of the future, the chance of encountering each second as "the straight gate through which the Messiah might enter."[21] From following traces to writing in the ashes—this is not only the trajectory of the concept of the archive in its burning-dreaming conceptualization. It is also the trajectory of the very figures of these burning conceptualizations, all these authors as themselves signs or dreaming figures.

THE FOOTSTEPS OF PSYCHOANALYSIS

> I too am dreaming.
>
> FRANCOISE DAVOINE, "The Characters of Madness
> in the Talking Cure"[22]

We may indeed perhaps read, by chance, emerging from the dream in Jensen, and repeated in Freud, the mark of a footprint. The first appearance of Gradiva in Pompeii is marked by a single word set off, typographically, in a separate line, a typographical separation that makes an immediate impression: "*plötzlich*," "suddenly":

> Hanold looked before him down the Strada di Mercurio . . .
> Then suddenly—
> With open eyes he gazed along the street, yet it seemed to him as if he were doing it in a dream. A little to the right something suddenly stepped forth . . . and across the lava stepping-stones, which led from the house to the other side of the Strada di Mercurio, Gradiva stepped buoyantly. (*G*, 48–50)

This word "suddenly" also appears in Hanold's first vision of Gradiva in his dream, and proliferates across Jensen's text and into Freud's after its appearance along with her image. "Suddenly" is, of course, the language of the unexpected, of the accident, of fright, of the event marked by trauma. It is also, here, the word of a chance meeting, an encounter that will also be, in Freud's reading, the beginning of a psychoanalytic process of encounter, or, we could say, the beginning of a certain kind of unprecedented witness. The "suddenly" thus emerges as an accident, mere chance, the beginning, perhaps, of a figure, and a future concept, but one that arises from and must always return to the dream, to the site of chance meetings and to the enigmatic language of the literary.[23] This word, then, emerging from the dream, may be the trace of the trauma, perhaps the footprint of Gradiva, or of psychoanalysis, as it leaves its footprints, [24] or as it may simply be disappearing, suddenly, imperceptibly, at the heart of its own burning, in the history of its writing, in the history of "today."

> If you never read this, no one will. . . . Or. Or perhaps no. Perhaps these words need the air that is out in the world. Need to fly up then fall, fall like ash over acres of primrose and mallow.[25]

Afterword

IN THE FINAL CHAPTER of this book, I turn to the encounter between Freud and a dream, the dream of the archaeologist Norbert Hanold that lies at the center of Wilhelm Jensen's novella *Gradiva: A Pompeiian Fantasy*. In this dream, the young archaeologist, who has become obsessed with a figure on a bas-relief he has purchased in Rome, finds himself in Pompeii on the day of the eruption of Vesuvius in AD 79 following a figure he believes to be that of the woman on the bas-relief, as she proceeds, step by step, to the place where she will lie down and be buried in the rain of ashes. Following her through the smoke and falling ashes in the dream, amid the anguished cries of the Pompeiians, Hanold wakes up with a new desire: to return to Pompeii to see if he can find the traces of her toe-print in the ash.

I have tried to show how, upon encountering this literary dream, Freud recognizes, with surprise, an image or a figure of his own theoretical discovery, the notion of the unconscious that he had, himself, likened to a buried city. But in this dream of ashes, in my interpretation, Freud also encounters a story about psychoanalysis at its own origins, a story that brings him back to a psychoanalytic past from before the theory of dreams, and at the same time points him forward, half consciously, toward the psychoanalytic future. It is a dream that bears witness to a new kind of history, the history of a trauma, as well as a dream that bears witness to the past, and to an as yet unknown future, of the traumatic history of psychoanalysis. It is thus a dream about the entanglement of history and psychoanalysis on the site of a catastrophe. In returning to the past, the dream is also a fable, or a fantasy, about the future, or rather a time when there may be no future, about a new time, or a new language, that emerges as a searching in the ash, *after the end*, for the traces of psychoanalysis and of history.

To search for traces in the ash: this is the story of an impossible quest, not for what lies buried beneath the ashes, but for what may be impossibly, evanescently, inscribed upon them. This is one of the most profound stories at the heart of psychoanalysis; and it is also, I argue, the unexhausted task and the legacy of Freud for our times. It is not a coincidence that this legacy defines itself, sketches out its contours, between and beyond the disciplines, beginning with the discovery of a literary text, and extending beyond the realm of psychoanalysis proper to the thinking of politics, philosophy, and literary theory in the twentieth and twenty-first centuries. In the various chapters of this book, in the writings of Honoré de Balzac, Hannah Arendt, Ariel Dorfman, Wilhelm Jensen, Sigmund Freud, and Jacques Derrida, we encounter, across different languages, a variety of narratives that bear witness not simply to the past but also to the pasts we have not known, and which, in so doing, repeatedly return us to a future that remains beyond imagination. For these stories of trauma cannot be limited to the catastrophes they name, and the theory of catastrophic history may ultimately be written in a language that already lingers, in these texts, after the end, in a time that comes to us from the other shore, from the other side of the disaster.

NOTES

Chapter One: Parting Words

1. *Beyond the Pleasure Principle*, in *The Standard Edition of the Complete Psychological Works of Sigmund Freud*, translated from the German under the general editorship of James Strachey in collaboration with Anna Freud, assisted by Alix Strachey and Jan Tyson, 24 vols. (London: Hogarth, 1953–74), chap. 2, xviii. German quotations are taken from Sigmund Freud, *Studienausgabe* (Frankfurt am Main: Fischer Verlag, 1969–79), vol. 3.

2. Freud describes the game as the child's "first great cultural achievement," and he suggests that the child rewarded himself for not expressing his distress by creating a game instead. Thus the game not only represents the mother's wished-for return, but by substituting itself for the mother the game becomes, itself, a kind of symbolic return.

3. The game has been read, for instance, as a game of mourning. Within the literary critical tradition, see, for example, Eric L. Santner, *Stranded Objects: Mourning, Memory, and Film in Postwar Germany* (New York: Cornell University Press, 1990). The received understanding of the game is that it represents a form of mastery and is thus, strictly speaking, not a purely traumatic repetition—unless traumatic repetition is understood as already a form of mastering. Freud does suggest at one point in his analysis that the game may express a principle of mastery "beyond the pleasure principle" but the peculiarity of such repetition is rarely explored within traditional analyses. An exception to this line of thought can be found in Jacques Derrida, "To Speculate—on 'Freud'" in *The Post Card: From Socrates to Freud and Beyond*, trans. Alan Bass (Chicago: University of Chicago Press, 1987). Jacques Lacan analyzes the game in the context of a reading of traumatic repetition in *The Four Fundamental Concepts of Psycho-Analysis*, trans. Alan Sheridan, ed. Jacques-Alain Miller (New York: W. W. Norton, 1978). See also Rodolphe Gasché, "The Witch Metapsychology," in *Returns of the French Freud: Freud, Lacan, and Beyond*, ed. Todd Dufresne (New York: Routledge, 1997). On the crucial structure of the game in relation to the speculative structure of *Beyond the Pleasure Principle*, see Samuel Weber, *The Legend of Freud* (Minneapolis: University of Minnesota Press, 1982), and his *Return to Freud: Jacques Lacan's Dislocation of Psychoanalysis*, trans. Michael Levine (Cambridge: Cambridge University Press, 1991).

4. For a related analysis of this aspect of Freud's text with a slightly different

emphasis, see my *Unclaimed Experience: Trauma, Narrative, and History* (Baltimore: Johns Hopkins University Press, 1996), chap. 3, "Traumatic Departures: Survival and History in Freud."

5. Ibid.

6. Life is thereby separated from the desire to live; survival is no longer linked to the wish to live but to another imperative that appears to have ethical force (thus the survivor mission to tell the story of the dead, or of a death encounter) as well as a relation to knowing and witnessing (as an "awakening").

7. The theory of individual trauma in *Beyond the Pleasure Principle* will, therefore, lead to the theory of historical (and collective) trauma in *Moses and Monotheism*. I have analyzed this in terms of the story of departure in *Unclaimed Experience*, chaps. 1 and 3. The notion of an attempt to return that becomes a departure is a pattern that originates in *Beyond the Pleasure Principle* in the description of individual trauma and ultimately the foundation of life; in *Moses and Monotheism*, Jewish history is structured by a trauma that turns Moses's attempt to return the Hebrews to Canaan into an endless departure into a Jewish history of survival.

8. Robert J. Lifton, "Survivor Experience and Traumatic Syndrome," in his *The Broken Connection: Death and the Continuity of Life* (1979; New York: Basic Books, 1983), 163–64.

9. Freud emphasizes the creative element of the game by remarking that it is the "first self-invented game" of the child (*das erste selbst-erschaffene Spiel*), an emphasis we see again in his letter to Wilhelm Zweig concerning his insight behind *Moses and Monotheism*, that "Moses created the Jews," which uses a related although slightly different verb form (*hat . . . geschaffen*). Freud's use of the word "create" in *Beyond the Pleasure Principle*, which I am echoing in my own use of the word "creative," thus has a specific, foundational meaning and is also, in both *Beyond the Pleasure Principle* and *Moses and Monotheism*, ultimately linked to a traumatic history. This creative element in the *fort/da* game appears, moreover, to be associated specifically with the origins of language; Freud notes that the game begins when the child is just beginning to make articulate sounds. Jacques Lacan suggests that this game represents the origin of symbolic language as such in the differentiation of the phonemes *o* and *a* (see his "Function and Field of Speech and Language," in *Écrits*, trans. Alan Sheridan [New York: W. W. Norton, 1977]). The game is not, that is, about symbolizing the literal but about moving from silence to speech. The foundational nature of the game—or of the scene as Freud presents it—points toward its link to the foundational moment that traumatic repetition repeats, which is the ultimate concern of *Beyond the Pleasure Principle*.

10. One line of theoretical (or in Freud's terms, "speculative") elaboration of the notion of trauma in *Beyond the Pleasure Principle* begins in chapter 2 with the example of the nightmares of battle, which are compared to the nightmares of an accident that wake the patient up from his sleep. This line of argument contin-

ues with the explanation of trauma in chapter 4, which speculates on the origins of consciousness and proposes that trauma is a break in the stimulus barrier that consciousness provides for the living organism. The argument culminates in chapter 5, in which Freud suggests that life itself was an awakening from inanimate matter for which there was no preparation. This line of speculation appears to have an independent logic and does not completely align itself with the language of play that accompanies it in an apparently separate line of argument. The *Spiel* appears first in the example of the child, is repeated in chapter 3 in regard to the reenactment behavior in transference, and thenceforth is mentioned only in regard to children's play and theater, until the introduction of the notion of the life drive in chapter 5. (Interestingly, the discussion of psychoanalytic treatment in chapter 3 suggests that the entire theory of the Oedipal origins of unconscious conflict in childhood needs to be rethought in relation to the notion of trauma; at this point in his argument, then, Freud appears to be incorporating the earlier theory of neurosis into a larger speculation concerning traumatic neurosis.)

It is notable that the distinction between the terminology of the nightmare (a terminology of seeing and awakening) and the terminology of the game (a language of play and speech) also appears in contemporary discussions of the movement from traumatic imagery to the resolution of trauma in (symbolic) language. See, for example, Bessel A. van der Kolk, "Trauma and Memory," in *Traumatic Stress: The Effects of Overwhelming Experience on Mind, Body, and Society*, ed. Bessel A. van der Kolk, Alexander C. McFarlane, and Lars Weisaeth (New York: Guilford Press, 1996).

11. The movement from the death drive to the life drive seems, in fact, to carry out a possibility contained in Freud's double denomination of trauma in chapter 2, as both fright (*Schreck*) and surprise (*Überraschung*): "*daß das Hauptgewicht der Verursachung auf das Moment der Überraschung, auf den Schreck, zu fallen schien.*" "*Schreck aber benennt den Zustand, in den man gerät, wenn man in Gefahr kommt, ohne auf sie vorbereitet zu sein, betont das Moment der Überraschung*" (222–23).

12. Interestingly, it is not until the introduction of the life drive that the *fort* makes its appearance again, in the language of Freud's text. Here we might see a possibility of bringing together Jean Laplanche's insight into the shared single energy of the life drive and death drive and Harold Bloom's insistence that Freud is a dualist. See Jean Laplanche, "Why the Death Drive?" in his *Life and Death in Psychoanalysis* (Baltimore: Johns Hopkins University Press, 1970), and Harold Bloom, "Freud's Concept of Defense and the Poetic Will," in his *Agon: Towards a Theory of Revisionism* (New York: Oxford University Press, 1982).

13. The repetition of the origin as the new beginning of the life drive thus distinguishes itself from the confusion between death and life enacted in the death drive. One thinks of the repeated confrontation with death in life that is associated, for example, with survivors' descriptions of themselves as the living dead (cf. Robert Lifton's *Death in Life: Survivors of Hiroshima* [New York: Basic Books, 1967]). Or we might turn to the literary example of the woman in Marguerite

Duras's and Alain Resnais's *Hiroshima mon amour* who, having missed the moment of her lover's death, exclaims, "I could not find the least difference between his dead body and mine." So too, in that film, the slap—which breaks the traumatic repetition in the woman's encounter with the Japanese man—can be understood as a new beginning that distinguishes death from life, a distinction that does not take the form of understanding but rather of an act. (See *Unclaimed Experience*, chap. 2.)

One might say that the event of trauma is repeated, in the moment of parting in the life drive, as the act of survival, an act that, in a sense, fulfills the imperative to live that begins life, but fulfills it differently (the imperative and its fulfillment are not continuous). This act of survival, though, is not just any act; since it repeats the "awakening" of the death drive, it is inextricable from the questions of witnessing or knowing that govern traumatic repetition (in so far as traumatic repetition can be traced to the origin of life and its awakening). The repetition that constitutes the life drive may consequently be understood as a different form of witnessing.

To this extent, the question of creativity—as a creativity arising in the context of trauma—is bound up with the question of truth. Rather than providing an affective response to trauma, the life drive can be understood as providing another means of bearing witness. In other words, the life drive (unlike, say, the pleasure principle) cannot be understood within the economy of pleasure (which is also the economy of symbolization, as we see in the *fort/da* game) but must rather engage the problems of truth and knowing introduced by trauma.

14. It should be noted that the passage from chapter 2 is already fairly complex and appears to be somewhat playful in its own use of *fort* and *da*, in naming the never-achieved pleasurable end of the game (the hoped-for *da*) as *"das zum lustvollen Ende fortgeführte Ganze"*—that is, in naming the longed-for *da* by means of a *fort*. The question of departure could also be thought in terms of a meditation on the nature of the return (Derrida suggests something of the sort in "To Speculate—on 'Freud' "); here it would be interesting to examine the shift from the *da* of the child—seen as the marker of the pleasure principle—to the *zurück* ("back," as in "to go back," or "return") of the drives beyond the pleasure principle. (For a discussion of different modes of return as they emerge from a reading of Freud, see chapters 4 and 5 of this book.)

The new meaning of *fortführen*, moreover, brings out a remarkable reversal that occurs in the movement from chapters 2 and 4 (where trauma is an exception to ordinary experience, an encounter with death that disturbs consciousness) to chapter 5 (where the traumatic delay defines the very origin of life itself, and ultimately, in its repetition in the life drive, the possibility of a new beginning). For whereas consciousness was understood, originally, to protect life against death (chapter 4), we can see (from chapter 5) that, since trauma reenacts an origin that marked the beginning of life, consciousness ultimately serves to protect the organism not from death but from life—or, more accurately, from the surprise of new beginnings.

15. Bernadette Leite, personal communication. She has spoken of this (and reiterated the importance of speaking) in the *Atlanta Journal-Constitution* (July 24, 1999 and August 15, 1999, among other dates). She was honored in the November 1999 edition of *Redbook*. Bernadette Leite worked for several years in association with the Minority Health Institute at the Rollins School of Public Health at Emory University. See also Stephen B. Thomas, Bernadette Leite, and Ted Duncan, "Breaking the Cycle of Violence among Youth Living in Metropolitan Atlanta: A Case History of Kids Alive and Loved," *Health Education & Behavior* 25, no. 2 (April 1998): 160.

16. As Greg says, "He called early, like 10 or 11. . . . But again, that was the night I went to my cousin's home; he called again, but I wasn't there." It should be noted that my use of the word "child" to describe Greg is based on my sense that Greg "grows up" in the encounter with Bernadette, in the moments of the interview in which he takes leave of his friend and of his former self. From this perspective, both his encounter with Bernadette and the child's game in Freud's text circle around the beginning of a new identity founded in the confrontation with loss. This interview was taped for the KAL project at the Emory School of Public Health.

17. The tone of Greg's language here might be understood as being achieved through a giving up of a certain kind of pathos, although, even in its humor, it attains a different pathos, perhaps the pathos of giving up pathos. I would like to thank Elizabeth Rottenberg for her insights into questions of humor and tone in the exchange between Greg and Bernadette Leite.

18. Peggy Phelan provides a brilliant and beautiful response to my reading of the *fort/da* game and the interview with Greg (in an earlier version of this chapter), as well as a wonderful analysis of the relation between Greg's game with Khalil and the game of the child in *Beyond the Pleasure Principle* as two forms of "gathering the remains of loss," in her moving essay, "Converging Glances: A Response to Cathy Caruth's 'Parting Words'," *Cultural Values* 5, no. 1 (January 2001): 27–40. I am grateful to Phelan's unique responsiveness to my writing in this piece and, in her words, to "what lies beyond its frame."

19. It is interesting to note that the language of departure and parting also arises at the end of the interview between Bernadette Leite and Greg: "B: Any parting words? G: Departing words? B: Parting words. . . . Words to say to others" (KAL Oral History Archive). For a crucial thinking of witness in the twentieth century, see Shoshana Felman and Dori Laub, *Testimony: Crises of Witnessing in Literature, Psychoanalysis and History* (New York: Routledge, 1991). Shoshana Felman's understanding of the performative dimension of witness might usefully be seen in relation to her earlier work, *The Scandal of the Speaking Body: Don Juan with J. L. Austin, or Seduction in Two Languages* (Stanford: Stanford University Press, 2002; originally published in French in 1980, first English publication as *The Literary Speech Act* by Cornell University Press in 1983).

20. Thus the future of Freud's text could be understood as a "beyond" in the

strict sense, both inside and outside of Freud's text, that is, as the language of a child inside the text (the language of the game as Freud describes it) and outside the text (the experience of the real child), a language (and child) that is already there but not yet there, in the same way the death and life drives, as forms of repetition, are already there and not yet there.

21. On the self-reflexive dimension of the scene, see, for example, Derrida, "Speculations—On 'Freud' "; on the self-reflexivity of *Beyond the Pleasure Principle*, see Harold Bloom, "Freud and the Sublime: A Catastrophe Theory of Creativity," in *Agon*, where he suggests that Freud's citation of Torquato Tasso in chapter 3 is "an allegory of Freud's own passage into the Sublime," and Perry Meisel, "Freud's Reflexive Realism," *October* 28 (Spring 1984). Freud's argument, as we have outlined, thus first appears to replace the notion of childhood Oedipal conflict with a notion of trauma modeled on the adult (war trauma), but the self-reflexive level of Freud's writing reintroduces the child's centrality or priority, though not as a concept but rather as a kind of language. From this perspective, the nature of the beginning constituted by the awakening at the origin of life could also be understood as a mode of origination bound up with (the potential for) language.

22. Thus Freud's own creative act could be said to arise (as in the interview between Greg and Bernadette) out of an encounter: his encounter with the child. The shift from death drive to life drive, which remains fairly enigmatic in its original speculative introduction in chapter 5—Freud simply breaks off the description of the death drive and starts up again with the life drive—could be said to take place on the level of the encounter (rather than as a logical part of an argument). In other words, if one were to ask, pragmatically or clinically, what would make possible the movement from death drive to life drive in an individual—what makes possible, for example, the language of the life drive for Greg—the answer would have to be found, in this particular text by Freud, on the level of the encounter, in the chance event of an encounter.

23. Not the distance of theoretical knowing, then, but the distance of the child's game.

24. On the *fort* at the origin, see Samuel Weber, *The Legend of Freud*, and Caruth, *Unclaimed Experience*, chap. 3.

25. As Freud insists in his own letters, *Beyond the Pleasure Principle* was mostly written before the death of Sophie and thus does not (in the strictest sense) refer directly to her death. By introducing Sophie's death in a footnote, however, Freud allows the event of her death to resonate in the text. This contributes to the parallel between the playing child, whose mother died after the game, and Freud, whose daughter Sophie died after the writing of Freud's text. On the death of Sophie, see, among others, Jacques Derrida, "Speculations—On 'Freud'," and Elisabeth Bronfen, "*Eine Frau verschwindet: Sophie Freud und* Jenseits des Lustprinzips," *Psyche* 47, no. 6 (January 1993). Anne Whitehead (in an unpublished

lecture) also remarks on the important contribution of Luce Irigaray to the un-read position of the mother in the *fort/da* game in "Belief Itself," in her *Sexes and Genealogies*, trans. Gillian C. Gill (New York: Columbia University Press, 1987).

26. The interweaving of language and history, once again, emerges in Freud's peculiar association of the death drive with something "unobtrusive" and, in later texts, "dumb," and the life drive with noise or "clamour." This distinction occurs first in *Beyond the Pleasure Principle* and is reiterated in *The Ego and the Id* and *Civilization and Its Discontents*. Reading the death drive in terms of its historical shape in *Beyond the Pleasure Principle* and *Moses and Monotheism*, we could say that what the language of the life drive bears witness to is, perhaps, the silence of history (or, in the child's game, the silence of the mother's departure).

27. To the extent that the life drive moves us away from the direct line of argu-ment that leads from *Beyond the Pleasure Principle* to *Moses and Monotheism*, or from individual to collective history, the imperative for survival could be un-derstood, here, as taking place within acts (or within the language of the life drive) that are neither simply individual nor simply collective (in the sense of those terms that preceded the death drive/life drive analysis). The introduction of the life drive in my argument can be understood, in this context, as the reintroduction of the notion of individual acts on the other side of the collective analysis of historical catastrophe. Here, the "individual" act (or the language of the life drive) might itself carry with it the force of a larger history.

On psychoanalysis and play, see D. W. Winnicott, *Playing and Reality* (Lon-don: Tavistock Publications, 1971). Here we might recall the importance of the word "create" for Freud discussed in note 9, and its passage into Winnicott in the notion of living creatively. It is also interesting to note that this later thinker of play was also interested, in this context, in the notion of surprise.

Chapter Two: The Claims of the Dead

1. Honoré de Balzac, *Le Colonel Chabert*, ed. Pierre Citron (Paris: French and European Publications, 1961); trans. Carol Cosman, under the title *Colonel Cha-bert* (New York, New Directions, 1997), 1–2; hereafter abbreviated CC. The text of *Le Colonel Chabert* underwent a number of revisions and appeared over the course of its writing under several different titles. I quote from the critical edition of the novel, which is based on the 1832 text with a few later modifications. I would like to give special thanks to Brian McGrath for his excellent research for this essay, and to Douglas Gould for his insights.

2. The italics are in Balzac's text and refer to the appeal being improvised aloud by one clerk, and "June 1814" is the answer another clerk gives when someone asks for the date. Pierre Gascar notes in his preface to his critical edition of the novel that the date of the decree that returns property to the aristocrats is some-what later (December 1814) than the date of the Charter (June 1814). Balzac had given the proper date for the decree in another text; it is possible that he wished,

here, to emphasize the link between the spirit of the Charter and the later decree concerning property. See Pierre Gascar, preface to *"Le Colonel Chabert" suivi de trois nouvelles,* ed. Patrick Berthier, 2nd ed. (Paris: Gallimard, 1974), 7–18.

3. Quoted in François Furet, *Revolutionary France 1770–1880,* trans. Antonia Nevill (Oxford: Wiley-Blackwell, 1995), 271. Article 11 of the Charter reads in French, "Toutes les recherches des opinions et votes émis jusqu' à la Restauration sont interdites. Le même oubli est commandé aux tribunaux et aux citoyens" (*Charter of 1814,* in J. P. T. Bury, *France 1814–1940* [London: Methuen, 1985], 301–2). The importance of forgetting is emphasized in the opening scene of the novel by the fact that the clerk, parodied in this scene, is repeatedly unable to remember the date of the Charter.

4. The legal legacy of the Revolution is understood to include, here, both the explicit attempts at codification of the law and the formalization of governmental and political organization contained in constitutions and charters; both of these dimensions of legal history were an ongoing and central concern in the post-Revolutionary decades.

5. The battle of Eylau was considered to have lost more officers than any other Napoleonic battle. The text Chabert refers to is an actual document that records the battle in detail. See Charles Theodore Beauvais de Preau, *Victoires, conquêtes, désastres, revers, et guerres civiles des Français de 1792 à 1815,* ed. Jacques Philippe Voïart and Ambroise Tardieu, 27 vols. (Paris, C. L. F. Panckoucke, 1817–22), vol. 17. The name "Chabert" does not appear to refer to an actual Chabert involved in this battle but may be based on a number of different figures from this period. See the critical editions of Citron and Gascar for speculation concerning the possible sources of this name.

6. Gascar presents this view clearly in his preface to the novel:

> The realism with which the war is presented here, a realism unprecedented in the history of literature, does not result simply from the sensibility of the writer who paints a picture of it. It is imposed on him by the novel aspect of armed confrontations. With Napoleon, that is to say with the utilization, thanks to conscription, of veritable human masses, with the progress of armaments . . . battles turn easily into carnage. Ten thousand Frenchmen fall at the battle of Eylau, in which Colonel Chabert takes part, and which led Napoleon to say, with crocodile tears, "This spectacle is made to inspire in princes the love of peace and the horror of war."
> (preface, 9–10, my translation)

On the profound effect of the outcome of the battle of Eylau on Napoleon, see Jean-Paul Kauffmann, *The Black Room at Longwood: Napoleon's Exile on Saint Helena,* trans. Patricia Clancy (New York: Four Walls Eight Windows, 1999).

7. On the notion of social death, see Orlando Patterson, *Slavery and Social Death: A Comparative Study* (Cambridge, Mass.: Harvard University Press, 1982). One of the fundamental concerns in the novel is the relation between the social

and the legal spheres as they became intertwined after the Revolution; property appears to be a point of linkage between the two realms and for this reason also links the formalities of the law to a realm not controlled by it. I am grateful to Michal Shaked for her insights into the legal significance of the right of property.

8. Napoleon's name was officially and legally attached to the Code in 1807 and removed twice later by the Charters of 1814 and 1830; in 1852 it was finally reinstated "'to pay homage to historical truth'" (Jean Carbonnier, "Le Code civil," in *Les Lieux de mémoire*, ed. Pierre Nora, 3 vols. [Paris: Gallimard, 1986], 2:296; see also Joseph Goy, "Civil Code," in *A Critical Dictionary of the French Revolution*, trans. Arthur Goldhammer, ed. François Furet and Mona Ozouf [Cambridge, Mass.: Belknap Press of Harvard University Press, 1989], 437–48). Napoleon's own sense of identification with the Code is expressed clearly in his proud words, "I have sown liberty lavishly wherever I have implanted *my* Civil Code" (quoted in Carbonnier, "Le Code civil," 2:2:299) and in his moving comment from St. Helena, "My true glory is not to have won forty battles; Waterloo will efface the memory of any number of victories. What nothing will efface, what will live eternally, is my Civil Code" (quoted in Goy, "Civil Code," 442). The history of war during the Napoleonic period is thus inextricable from the history of law, a perplexing entanglement of law and violent conquest that Napoleon himself attempts to idealize in his monumentalization of the Code after his political exile.

9. On the exemplary status of compromise as a legal principle, see Martin Shapiro, "Compromise and Litigation," in *Compromise in Ethics, Law, and Politics*, ed. J. Roland Pennock and John W. Chapman (New York: New York University Press, 1979), 163–75.

10. The definition of property in the Code would appear to determine this negotiability in terms of the possessibility of property. The full definition reads: "Property is the right of enjoying and disposing of things in the most absolute manner, provided they are not used in a way prohibited by the laws or statutes" (*The Code of Napoleon; or, The French Civil Code*, trans. by a Barrister of the Inner Temple [London: Thomas Davison, 1824]). This definition has led to many interpretations of the Code's mechanistic qualities, which are associated with Napoleon's dictatorial aims or the nature of imperial bourgeois society. See, for example, Jean-Louis Halpérin, *Histoire du droit privé français depuis 1804* (Paris: Presses Universitaires de France, 1996); see also Elisabeth Sledziewski, *Révolutions du sujet* (Paris: Méridiens Klincksieck,1989), and Xavier Martin, "Nature humaine et Code Napoléon," *Droits*, no. 2 (1985): 177–228.

However, the Code is also interpreted by some scholars as a compromise between competing notions of property that inscribes in it a history of the complexity and enigma of this notion. See, for example, Jacques Poumerade, "De la difficulté de penser la propriété (1789–1793)," in *Propriété et Révolution*, ed. Geneviève Koubi (Paris: Éd. du Centre national de la recherche scientifique; Toulouse: Université de Toulouse I, Service des publications, 1990), 27–42. Koubi analyzes what she calls the "ideological breach" in the notion of property at the heart of the *Declaration*, a breach signaled by the use of the singular term "property" and the plural term "properties" in articles 2 and 17, respectively. These two terms are associated, in her analysis, with notions of liberty, on the one hand, and power on the other. See her "De l'article 2 à l'article 17 de la *Déclaration* de 1789: La 'Brèche' dans le discours révolutionnaire," in *Propriété et revolution*, 65–84. Balzac's story indeed appears to center, in part, around the plurality of notions of property contained in the legal use of the word. Chabert's apparent identification of selfhood and property might perhaps be seen in terms of what Etienne Balibar calls the "juridical" (as opposed to economic) notion of property, the right to property that is very closely tied to a right to one's person and the right to oneself and one's labor, or what Margaret Jane Radin refers to as nonfungible property. See Etienne Balibar, "What Is a Politics of the Rights of Man?," in *Masses, Classes, Ideas: Studies on Politics and Philosophy before and after Marx*, trans. James Swenson (New York: Routledge, 1994), 205–25, and Margaret Jane Radin, "Property and Personhood," *Stanford Law Review* 34 (May 1982): 957–1015.

For an analysis of the movement from earlier to later meanings of property in post-Revolutionary law, see Sledziewski, *Révolutions du sujet*, who provides a remarkable analysis of what she calls "slippage" in the notion of property from the *Declaration* to the Civil Code, which also accounts for the more reduced economic model in the Code. In her analysis, the slippage occurs because of the inherent tension between the subject as giver and receiver of the law arising in the self-declaration of 1789; this played itself out, historically, in the varying interpretations of property in the 1790s, during the repeated formulation of declarations and constitutions up until the Civil Code (and passed on, then, presumably, to the Restoration). On the complexity of the problem of codification in this period, see also Jean-Louis Halpérin, *L'Impossible code civil* (Paris: Presses Universitaires de France, 1992). Several critics analyze the problem of property in terms of debates concerning Lockean and Rousseauist interpretations as they played themselves out over time. See Florence Gauthier, "L'Idée générale de propriété dans la philosophie du droit naturel et la contradiction entre liberté politique et liberté économique 1789–1795," in *La Révolution et l'ordre juridique privé—Rationalité ou scandle?*, 2 vols. ([Orléans?]: CNRS, Université d'Orléans; [Paris]: P.U.F., 1988), 1:161–71, and Chantal Gaillard, *La Révolution de 1789 et la propriété: La Propriété attaquée et sacralisée* (Paris: Ecole des hautes études en sciences sociales, 1991).

11. The relation between the two characters that Derville attempts to establish, when he treats them as if they were two equal human beings before the law, thus harbors within it another kind of nonsymmetrical relation between someone not yet a person (Chabert) and someone already established as human (Mme. Ferraud). It is the difficulty of articulating the latter asymmetry with the need of the law for the symmetrical recognition between two parties that could be said to determine, in part, the development of the plot as it proceeds from this point.

12. In Sledziewski's words, the *Declaration* founds the "citizen-man" as "a juridical figure of individuality": "The individual as the locus of right, that is to say, as the place where the law founds itself in right, and where subjective aspiration becomes right, requires the law: that is indeed the invention of the Revolution" (Sledziewski, *Révolutions du sujet*, 27). Balibar further notes that this is associated specifically with the "'imprescriptible'" right to property, which thus defines this subject "in its essential characteristics" and hence *constitutes* it precisely as proprietor ("What Is a Politics?," 217). On the mutual "witnessing" permitted by the "auto-declaration" of right, see Claude Lefort, *Democracy and Political Theory*, trans. David Macey (Minneapolis: University of Minnesota Press, 1988).

13. Balzac would appear, in this scene, to put on stage not only the two characters but also the highly theatrical language used by historians of the period to describe the Revolution; it is not only the artifice of the literary text but the language of historians that Derville thus imitates.

14. Carbonnier writes beautifully of the Code as a place of memory in "Le Code Civil." (For a broader discussion of "lieux de mémoire," see Nora, "Between Memory and History: *Les Lieux de mémoire*," *Representations*, no. 26 [Spring 1989]: 7–25.) On the relation between the founding act of declaration and the difficulties for a codified system to reflect the performative dimension of such an act, see Keith Michael Baker, "Fixing the French Revolution," in *Inventing the French Revolution: Essays on French Political Culture in the Eighteenth Century* (Cambridge: Cambridge University Press, 1990), 253–54, who writes illuminatingly on the double notion of constitution as both "institution" and "order" that operated in post-Revolutionary discussions. Thomas Keenan's important discussion of the founding act of the Revolution and, more broadly, of the claim to rights, has been crucial to my thinking of the subject; see *Fables of Responsibility: Aberrations and Predicaments in Ethics and Politics* (Stanford: Stanford University Press, 1997), chap. 1, "Left to Our Own Devices: On the Impossibility of Justice," 7–42. See also Jacques Derrida, "Declarations of Independence," trans. Thomas Keenan and Tom Pepper, *New Political Science* 15 (Summer 1986): 7–15.

15. Balzac's narrator uses the phrase "*abyss of the Revolution*" in reference to the words of Louis XVI, in the course of describing Monsieur Ferraud's personal history and his own relation to the revolutionary past (CC, 58). It is notable that the Revolution in French historiography will sometimes be described as an "enigma" (Lefort, *Democracy and Political Theory*, 37) or a rupture, or as an event not in time; see, for example, Furet and Ozouf, preface, *A Critical Dictionary of the French Revolution*, xiii–xxii.

16. The restriction of women's rights in the Code, a regression from Revolutionary principles, is generally associated with Napoleon's own views of women. It is clear that Mme. Ferraud's manipulation of the inheritance and her husband's holdings is not only a matter of greed but also an exercise of rights that had in fact been limited by imperial law; in this sense, she too, like Chabert, is attempting to create herself and survive as a subject. Interestingly, Napoleon also said there

was no place for "bastards" in society and restricted their inheritance rights; given Chabert's status as an orphan, this places him, as well as Mme. Ferraud, in a marginal position in the world of the Civil Code. On these matters, see Halpérin, *Histoire du droit privé français depuis 1804*.

17. Colonel Chabert and Mme. Ferraud are frequently interpreted in the critical literature as allegorical figures representing the Empire and the Restoration, respectively, and are likewise subjected to value judgments (Chabert's positive, Mme. Ferraud's negative). Such interpretations neglect the peculiar in-between status of these characters and the way in which history, in this text, appears to take place in the interstices between actual periods. See, for example, Graham Good, "*Le Colonel Chabert*: A Masquerade with Documents," *French Review* 42 (May 1969): 846–56, and Eileen B. Sivert, "Who's Who: Non-Characters in *Le Colonel Chabert*," *French Forum* 13 (May 1988): 217–28.

18. In the scene in which Derville first convinces Mme. Ferraud to agree to a compromise, she asks if Chabert still loves her; this question, the narrator tells us, appears to indicate the seeds of a plan to use the meeting at the lawyer's office to manipulate Chabert. In this sense the theatrical gesture of Derville is already overtaken by the theatrical gesture of Mme. Ferraud. But behind this theatrical gesture, too—or under the costume that she wears—Mme. Ferraud, like Chabert, operates from an abyssal past.

19. Balibar, "What Is a Politics of the Rights of Man?," 217.

20. In this sense, Balzac's text appears to suggest a way in which the history of the Code remains in excess of the Code: it is an aspect of the Code's own foundation and unfolding that is not available to it in its civil function as a form of memory. This is not a history, in other words, that could be captured by the Code's implicit representation of its past. It might be appropriate, in this context, to think of Hannah Arendt's analysis of the "rightless"—those who emerge, after the institution of civil law, not simply as individuals whose rights have not been adequately respected but as a group who lie entirely outside the realm of rights—which is a phenomenon that only emerges, she says, in a world dominated by civil government. See Hannah Arendt, *The Origins of Totalitarianism* (New York: Harcourt, Brace & World, 1951). On the muteness of those excluded from the law as a place of speech, see Jean-François Lyotard, "The Other's Rights," trans. Chris Miller and Robert Smith, in *On Human Rights: The Oxford Amnesty Lectures 1993*, ed. Stephen Shute and Susan Hurley (New York: Basic Books, 1993), 135–47.

21. Balzac's story in many ways appears to anticipate the structure of repetition (or more precisely, repetition compulsion) as Freud formulated it in *Beyond the Pleasure Principle* one hundred years after these events and after another catastrophic war. See Sigmund Freud, *Beyond the Pleasure Principle*, in *The Standard Edition of the Complete Psychological Works of Sigmund Freud*, trans. and ed. James Strachey, 24 vols. (London, Hogarth Press, 1953–74), 18:7–64. Chabert's repeated "deaths" in his attempt to come before the law, in particular in the scene

in Derville's office, could be understood as the repetition of an ungrasped historical event much like the repeated event of a missed death described by Freud. In many ways, Balzac's story could be said to anticipate Freud's work, not so much in its psychological as in its historical dimensions. *Beyond the Pleasure Principle* would indeed be rethought, in historical terms, in *Moses and Monotheism*, and one might also read Freud's postwar work, in light of this French literary history, as a larger cultural reflection on a revolutionary history still reverberating throughout Europe. See Freud, *Moses and Monotheism*, in *The Standard Edition of the Complete Psychological Works of Sigmund Freud*, 23:3–137. Interestingly, shortly before the end of Balzac's novel, Chabert is compared to the women at the Salpêtrière; the Salpêtrière was, of course, the French hospital in which Freud encountered the study of hysterical women and then proceeded, in the following years, to develop his early theory of trauma.

22. An exception to the readings in which Chabert is associated with the good old days of the Empire is the analysis by Peter Brooks, who reads the encounter between Chabert and Derville on the model of a psychoanalytic encounter. In this interpretation the function of Derville is to allow Chabert to work through his loss of the past in order to enter and move forward in the present. This reading has the virtue of recognizing the impossibility of Chabert's claim, an impossibility connected with the absoluteness and irreversibility of events. However, Brooks proceeds, on the basis of this interpretation of the story, to read the final part of the novel as a kind of failure, which he associates with the dangers of narrative; he does not consider the legal and philosophical (or human) significance of the structural position of the final scenes of the book and the final verbal acts of Chabert. See Peter Brooks, "Narrative Transaction and Transference (Unburying *Le Colonel Chabert*)," *Novel* 15 (Winter 1982): 101–10.

23. Insofar as this scene repeats the earlier scenes of failure, which is itself a repetition of earlier "deaths," one might understand it as anticipating the kind of movement that, in *Beyond the Pleasure Principle*, occurs between the repetition compulsion of the death drive and the peculiar, originary, and originating repetition that emerges from it. While we would not want to make too close an analogy between the structure of the plot in Balzac and the structure of repeated repetitions in Freud, there is nonetheless a principle of opening that is shared by both and is crucial, I believe, to their historical significance. On the law as the site of historical reenactment and witness, see the innovative readings of twentieth-century trials in Shoshana Felman, *The Juridical Unconscious: Trials and Traumas in the Twentieth Century* (Cambridge, Mass.: Harvard University Press, 2002).

24. Much of the difficulty with historical movement is played out, in the novel, on the level of names. Thus Mme. Ferraud's peculiar temporal position is reflected in the split between her two names, Mme. Chabert and Mme. Ferraud; Colonel Chabert emerges as Hyacinthe; and, as previously noted, the Civil Code reflected a split between its legal and historical dimensions in its being referred to as both the Civil Code and the Napoleonic Code. The relation between names and prop-

erty would be important to examine in this light; Chabert's act of renaming himself as Hyacinthe is no longer associated, as was his attempt to reclaim the name Chabert, with the claiming of possessions.

25. On the act of renunciation (and promise), see Hannah Arendt, *The Human Condition*, 2nd ed. (1958; Chicago: University of Chicago Press, 1998), sec. 5, "Action," 175–247. Although one would not want to give too much contextual weight to the promise in the scene, it does, perhaps, allow for a link between Chabert's new act and the old legal one that he is, in a sense, giving up. In addition to recalling the centrality of the promise in the *Social Contract*, generally considered to be one of the philosophical sources of the Revolution, Chabert's act draws on the power of the speech act constituted by the 1789 *Declaration*. On the significance of such an originary linguistic gesture, see Keenan, *Fables of Responsibility*, and Derrida, "Declarations of Independence." Christine Fauré also discusses the centrality of the performative utterance to the *Declaration* in her preface to her edition of *Les Déclarations des droits de l'homme de 1789*, ed. Christine Fauré (Paris: Éditions Payot, 1988), 15–37. Lefort, in *Democracy and Legal Theory*, notes the "enigma" that the *Declaration* makes of "both humanity and right" by reducing the source of right to an utterance of right (37).

26. Emmanuel Levinas, *Difficult Freedom: Essays on Judaism*, trans. Seán Hand (Baltimore: Johns Hopkins University Press, 1990), 199. What Levinas describes here and what Chabert appears to enact might be thought of as a relation to history that is not subject to what Balibar calls "the principle of total possession," the assumption according to which all property, he argues, has previously been understood ("What Is a Politics?," 219).

27. Chabert is first seen by Derville in a court and then a prison following his conviction as a vagabond, then once again, accidentally, on the road, as he is passing by the almshouse, and finally when Derville returns to the almshouse with Godeschal (all sightings that occur, interestingly, *after* the novel states, "Chabert, in fact, disappeared" [*CC*, 91]—a sentence that could be read in terms of the name "Chabert"). The surprising recognition of Chabert's face recalls the earliest scenes of surprise—in Balzac's text, the description of Chabert's face in the first encounter with Derville involves an extended and lengthy development—but with the difference that Chabert's face is now described as noble, rather than as ghastly or ghostly. The emphasis on Chabert's disfigured face, in this story, has intriguing implications for the relations among property, identity, and the body as well as for the ethical dimension implicit in the address of the unrecognizable other.

28. On the future-oriented, prophetic element of Balzac's writing, see Walter Benjamin, *The Arcades Project*, trans. Howard Eiland and Kevin McLaughlin (Cambridge, Mass.: Belknap Press of Harvard University Press, 1999). Balzac's inscription of an allusion to the novelist in Derville's final comments, in this scene of teaching, may also reflect his own passage from his training as law clerk to that of literary writer, and what was passed on in the movement from one mode of writing to the other.

Chapter Three: Lying and History

1. Hannah Arendt, *The Human Condition* (Chicago: University of Chicago Press, 1998), 177–178. I would like to thank Jennifer Orth for her research assistance on Hannah Arendt.

2. Ibid., 207.

3. Ibid., 8–9.

4. Hannah Arendt, "Truth and Politics," in *Between Past and Future* (New York: Penguin Books, 1954), 236 (hereafter cited in text as TP).

5. Freud's extended analysis of this phenomenon is to be found in *Beyond the Pleasure Principle*, in *The Standard Edition of the Complete Psychological Works of Sigmund Freud*, ed. James Strachey (London: Hogarth, 1963–74), vol. 18.

6. For an excellent analysis of deception in Arendt, see Peg Birmingham, "A Lying World Order: Deception and the Rhetoric of Terror," *Good Society* 16, no. 2 (2007): 32–37.

7. For an analysis of the performative dimension of the lie and its relation to historicity in Arendt (and others), see Jacques Derrida, "History of the Lie: Prolegomena," in *Without Alibi*, ed. Peggy Kamuf (Stanford: Stanford University Press, 2002), 28–70. See also Peggy Kamuf's incisive introduction to *Without Alibi*. A different and excellent consideration of deception in Arendt may be found in Peg Birmingham, "A Lying World Order: Political Deception and the Threat of Totalitarianism," in *Thinking in Dark Times: Hannah Arendt on Ethics and Politics*, ed. Roger Berkowitz, Jeffrey Katz, and Thomas Keenan (New York: Fordham University Press, 2010).

8. Hannah Arendt, *The Origins of Totalitarianism* (New York: Harcourt Brace, 1976), 262.

9. Ibid., 252–53.

10. Hannah Arendt, "Lying in Politics," in *Crises of the Republic* (New York: Harcourt Brace, 1972), 4 (hereafter cited in text as LP).

11. It should be noted that Arendt is in part responding, in her essay, to Daniel Ellsberg's own analysis of the Pentagon Papers in his essay "The Quagmire Myth and the Stalemate Machine," which had been published earlier; its final version appears in his *Papers on the War* (New York: Simon & Schuster, 1972). In this essay, Ellsberg describes a "stalemate machine" at the heart of the war process that oscillates between deception and self-deception on the part of the government; Arendt argues, on the contrary, that "the deceivers started with self-deception."

12. There is interesting work on the atomic bomb and its effects in relation to the images it produced as well as the kind of technology invented in order to make images of it. One interesting book on the former topic is Akira Mizuta Lippit's *Atomic Light (Shadow Optics)* (Minneapolis: University of Minnesota Press, 2005). See also Peter Kuran, *How to Photograph an Atomic Bomb* (VCE, 2007).

13. Arendt, *Origins of Totalitarianism*, 478.

14. Ibid., 267.

15. On half-erasure in a literary context, see Paul de Man, "Shelley Disfigured," *The Rhetoric of Romanticism* (New York: Columbia University Press, 1984).

16. Ellsberg, *Papers on the War*, 36.

17. It is interesting that Neil Sheehan, a reporter who published the Pentagon Papers articles in the *New York Times* and then later published a book compilation of them, said that reading them the first time "was like an explosion going off in our mind" ("Remembering the Viet Nam War: Conversation with Neil Sheehan," interviewer Harry Kreisler, University of California at Berkeley, Institute of International Studies, available online at http://globetrotter.berkeley.edu/conversations/Sheehan/sheehan-conO.html).

18. Daniel Ellsberg, "Secrecy Oaths: A License to Lie?" *Harvard International Review* 26, no. 2 (2004): 16–19.

19. Ellsberg, *Papers on the War*, 80.

Chapter Four: Disappearing History

1. Ariel Dorfman, *Death and the Maiden* (New York: Penguin Books, 1991), cast and setting page [play hereafter cited as *DM*]. The translation is by Ariel Dorfman. The Spanish differs significantly, in some passages, from the English, some aspects of which I will discuss further on in the essay. For the Spanish version (a revised version of the original Spanish text written after the appearance of the play in English), see Ariel Dorfman, *La Muerte y La Doncella* (New York: Siete Cuentos Editorial, 1992), hereafter cited as *MD*. Information concerning the translation into English and the rewriting of the Spanish come from Ariel Dorfman, personal communication. It should be noted that the following essay does not concern Roman Polanski's film version of the play, *Death and the Maiden*, which makes some significant changes. I would like to thank Ariel Dorfman for his generous communications with me concerning the genesis of his text. Mary Luckhurst provided important comments on an early draft of this chapter, for which I am grateful. I would also like to thank Ronald Mendoza-De Jesus, Armando Mastrogiovanni, and Gustavo Llarull for outstanding research assistance.

2. See the *Report of the Chilean National Commission on Truth and Reconciliation* (United Sates Institute of Peace, www.usip.org), Spanish version available at http://www.derechoschile.com/english/resour.htm. The Commission was meant to investigate crimes in relation to the dead and disappeared but not the living; the Commission also recommended reparations, but their recommendations did not have binding force with regard to judicial matters. The use of the word "disappeared" is generally considered to have gained wide use in a new transitive form during this period, though the word also appears in its intransitive uses as well in this report, as elsewhere. On the use of the term "disappeared" (*desaparecido/a*), see Marguerite Feitlowitz, *A Lexicon of Terror: Argentina and the Legacies of Torture* (Oxford: Oxford University Press, 1998). She notes that the term was invented in its transitive form by the Argentine military in order to cover up its crimes (see the use by Videla and note 11).

3. "The Commission's task was to draw up as complete a picture as possible of the most serious human rights violations that resulted in death and disappearances which were committed by government agents or by private citizens for political purposes; to gather evidence that would make it possible to identify individual victims and determine their fate or whereabouts; to recommend such measures of reparation and restoration of people's good name as it regarded as just, and also to recommend measures that should be adopted to hinder or prevent new violations from being committed" (*Report of the Chilean National Commission on Truth and Reconciliation*).

4. Paulina repeatedly says that she wants to put Roberto on trial (this is translated from the verb *juzgar*, "to try" or "to judge"). She is also clearly reenacting aspects of her torture, thus juxtaposing the staging of the trial and that of the torture, which may be mixed in her mind (since the Commission and possible trials exclude her and hence deprive her of her rights as well). The Commission's proceedings were not a trial, so one might alternatively read the desire for the trial not only in relation to what she does not have the right to do in relation to the Commission but also what the Commission does not have the right to do under its own charter.

5. The play marks a "transitional" moment in the return to democracy, and deals with what is now called "transitional justice." One of the questions at stake here is the relation between the laws that pertain to a democratic state and laws concerning human rights in general. Dorfman, himself, emphasizes the importance of the transitional moment when he speaks about the play (see, for example, his "Afterword" to *Death and the Maiden*). We might consider the question of what constitutes a "transitional" moment in legal discourse. With regard to the "human rights" claim of the report, it says that "the human rights policy, therefore, rested mainly on disclosing the truth" (*Report of the Chilean National Commission on Truth and Reconciliation*). For an excellent discussion of the history and nature of "transitional justice," see Ruth G. Teitel, "Transitional Justice Genealogy," *Harvard Human Rights Journal* 16 (2003): 69–94, and *Transitional Justice* (Oxford: Oxford University Press, 2000). See also *Trauma and Memory: Reading, Healing, and Making Law*, ed. Austin Sarat, Nadav Davidovitch, and Michal Alberstein (Stanford: Stanford University Press, 2007).

6. As noted earlier, the Chilean truth and reconciliation commission was limited to examination of the dead and disappeared who did not return. On the various forms of transitional justice in different countries during the Dirty Wars, see Edward L. Cleary, *The Struggle for Human Rights in Latin America* (Westport, Conn.: Praeger, 1997); Mark Ensalaco, "Truth Commissions for Chile and El Salvador: A Report and Assessment," *Human Rights Quarterly* 16 (1994): 656–75; Greg Grandin and Thomas Miller Klubock, eds., "Truth Commissions: State Terror, History, and Memory," special issue, *Radical History Review*, no. 97 (2007); Brian Grodsky, "Re-ordering Justice: Towards a New Methodological Approach to Studying Transitional Justice," *Journal of Peace Research* 46, no. 6 (2009):

819–37; Jaime Malamud-Goti, *Game without End: State Terror and the Politics of Justice* (Norman: University of Oklahoma Press, 1996); David Weissbrodt and Paul W. Fraser, "Book Review: Report of the Chilean National Commission on Truth and Reconciliation," *Human Rights Quarterly* 14, no.4 (1992); and Thomas C. Wright, *State Terrorism in Latin America: Chile, Argentina, and International Human Rights* (Lanham, Md.: Rowman and Littlefield, 2007).

7. The setting, as it is given in English, is "the time is the present and the place, a country that is probably Chile but could be any country that has given itself a democratic government just after a long period of dictatorship" (*DM*, cast and setting page). It is interesting to note that the Spanish version is somewhat less certain about the democratic achievement: "El tiempo es el presente; y el lugar, un país que es probablemente Chile, aunque puede tratarse de cualquier país que acaba de salir de una dictadura" [The time is the present; and the place, a country that is probably Chile, although it could be any country that has just come out of a dictatorship] (*MD*, 11). For an interesting article on the notion of transition in relation to a traumatic history, see Idelber Avelar, "Five Theses on Torture," *Journal of Latin American Cultural Studies* 10, no. 3 (2001): 253–71. This text also engages in a critique of the film version of the play.

8. We might interpret this problem as legal, societal, cultural and psychological.

9. Gerardo says to Paulina, "[L]ook at you, love. You're still a prisoner, you stayed there behind with them, locked in that basement. For fifteen years you've done nothing with your life. Not a thing. Look at you, just when we've got the chance to start all over again and you begin to open all the wounds" (*DM*, 38). It is important to keep in mind that the psychological explanation of Paulina's "symptoms" is represented by one of the characters who is part of the larger performance; one would thus want to be careful about attributing a pathological version of trauma to Paulina. Although a number of critics have interpreted the Paulina character as traumatized—either to examine the notion of trauma or to denigrate the text as making her into a destabilized victim—the position that insists on her traumatization, in the play, is explicitly problematized. For this reason (among others) we should note that "trauma" in the play is staged, to the extent that, as a collective phenomenon, it encompasses all three figures. On trauma in the play, see Nora Glickman, "Los gritos silenciados en el teatro de Aída Bortnik, Alberto Adellach, Eduardo Pavlovsky y Ariel Dorfman," *Revista Hispánica Moderna* 50, no. 1 (June 1997): 180–89; Manuel Alcídes Jofre, "*La muerte y la doncella*, de Ariel Dorfman: Transición democrática y crisis de la memoria," *Atenea: Revista de ciencia, arte y literatura*, no. 429 (Fall 1994): 87–99; Gabriele Schwab, *Haunting Legacies: Violent Histories and Transgenerational Trauma* (New York: Columbia University Press, 2010); Lizabeth Lira, "Remembering: Passing Back through the Heart," in *Collective Memory of Political Events: Social and Psychological Perspectives*, ed. James W. Pennebaker, Dario Páez, and Bernard Rimé

(Mahwah, N.J.: Lawrence Erlbaum, 1997), 223–36. I would like to draw particular attention to the work of Henry James Morello, *Masking the Past: Trauma in Latin American and Peninsular Theatre* (Ph.D. diss., University of Illinois, Urbana-Champaign, 2006)—he speaks interestingly of a "post-traumatic theater" in Latin America, and provides, within this context, an astute reading of *Death and the Maiden*.

10. On the question of transitional justice in Chile, see Cath Collins, *Post-Transitional Justice: Human Rights Trials in Chile and El Salvador* (Pittsburgh: Penn State University Press, 2011).

11. *Military Junta: Basic Documents and Political Foundations of the Armed Forces in the "Proceso de Reorganización Nacional"* (Buenos Aires: La Junta, 1980). Cited in Nicole M. Diaz, "The Politics of Nomenclature: An Analysis of Language in Government Speeches, Laws and Popular Discourse in Argentina from 1976–2007" (senior thesis, Emory University, 2009). Also available in Spanish on Youtube (see http://www.youtube.com/watch?v=9MPZKG4Prog). I am grateful for the brilliant work of Nicole Diaz in her senior thesis, which is the origin of my own interest in the "disappeared."

With regard to Videla's strange wording, my student Gustavo Llarull notes that the phrase translated here as "he has no age" is, in Spanish, "*no tiene entidad*," literally "he has no entity." Gustavo has been tremendously helpful in clarifying the complexities of the Spanish in this speech as well as in Dorfman's text and in providing details about the Dirty Wars in Chile and in Argentina.

12. See Hannah Arendt, "Truth and Politics," in *Between Past and Future* (New York: Penguin Books, 1954), and Hannah Arendt, "Lying in Politics," in *Crises of the Republic* (New York: Harcourt Brace, 1972). On the notion of the "modern lie" in these essays, see chapter 3 of this book.

13. See Hannah Arendt, *The Origins of Totalitarianism* (New York: Harcourt Brace, 1976). An astute commentary on this notion can be found in Thomas Keenan, "Left to Our Own Devices: On the Impossibility of Justice," in his *Fables of Responsibility: Aberrations and Predicaments in Ethics and Politics* (Stanford: Stanford University Press, 1997). He also writes here of the strange "survival" of rights discourse beyond its apparent demise, a notion of survival that might be thought in interesting ways with other kinds of survival in this play.

14. On the notion of "law," see note 5.

15. Sigmund Freud, *Beyond the Pleasure Principle*, in *The Standard Edition of the Complete Psychological Works of Sigmund Freud,* translated from the German under the general editorship of James Strachey in collaboration with Anna Freud, assisted by Alix Strachey and Alan Tyson, 24 vols. (London: Hogarth, 1953–74), vol. 18.

16. Freud might be interpreted here as producing a theory of performance. On performance and disappearance, see Peggy Phelan's brilliant essay, "The Ontology of Performance: Representation without Reproduction," in her *Unmarked: The*

Politics of Performance (New York: Routledge, 1993), where she says that performance "becomes itself through disappearance." On the *fort/da* and Freud's own performance in relation to that of the child, see chapter 1 of this book. On performance, disappearances, and the Dirty War in Argentina, see Diana Taylor, *Disappearing Acts: Spectacles of Gender and Nationalism in Argentina's "Dirty War"* (Durham, N.C.: Duke University Press, 1997). See also Diana Taylor, *The Archive and the Repertoire: Performing Cultural Memory in the Americas* (Durham, N.C.: Duke University Press, 2003).

17. By disappearance I do not mean that the event was literally not recorded by anyone, but rather that elements of the event as a whole were not integrated into the society or law, as the play represents it.

18. For example:

Roberto: You are exactly what this country needs, to be able to find out the truth once and for all. . . .

Gerardo: What the country needs is justice, but if we can determine at least part of the truth. . . .

Roberto: Just what I was about to say. Even if we can't put these people on trial, even if they're covered by this amnesty they gave themselves—at least their names can be published.

Gerardo: Those names are to be kept secret. The Commission is not supposed to identify the authors of crimes or—

Roberto: In this country everything finally comes out into the open.
. . . .

Gerardo: . . . we all know these people [the military and their supporters] are ready to jump on us at the slightest mistake we make. . . .

Roberto: Well, that was exactly my point, when you said that the names wouldn't be known, published . . . —maybe you're right, maybe we'll finally never know who these people really were . . . It may not be as easy as I thought. . . .

Gerardo: Not that difficult either. . . . And once people start talking, once the confessions begin, the names will pour out like water. Like you said: in this country we end up knowing everything.

Roberto: I wish I could share your optimism. I'm afraid there are things we'll never know. (*DM*, 15–17)

It is also interesting to note that it is Roberto who introduces a language of guilt and apology in this conversation, as well as the question of the "real real truth" of his being at the house at midnight, which does not arouse the curiosity of Gerardo and is, indeed, taken over by Gerardo as well in his own ensuing apologies to Roberto for his own and his wife's rudeness. The frequent use of "*perdon*" throughout the text would also bear additional scrutiny.

19. We might say that the mark of the knocking is turned into a sign by Ge-

rardo, which elicits a story that nonetheless reenacts something unknown within it (as we might say also about the movement from the "o-o-o" of the child in Freud whose story becomes a *"fort,"* then a *"fort da,"* then a *"fort"*). Here, however, the performance is specifically the performance of the "modern lie."

20. Thus Paulina's action can be said to be inscribed in their action, or called up by it. Gerardo, indeed, invites Roberto to stay the night in order to meet Gerardo's wife.

21. I have modified the English, here, to reflect the Spanish "that you played for me" [*que usted me tocó*].

22. It should be noted that some critics assume that the audience will interpret Paulina as being mad. See, for example, Idelber Avelar, who is interpreting the movie but, in this context, refers to aspects of the play as well: Idelber Avelar, "*La muerte y la doncella* o la hollywoodización de la tortura," *Revista de crítica cultural*, no. 22 (2001): 21–23.

23. The relation between truth and justice is not simple in this play. For a profound reading of related problems of speech, performance, and justice in the context of the Adolf Eichmann trial, see Shoshana Felman, "A Ghost in the House of Justice: Death and the Language of the Law," in her *The Juridical Unconscious: Trials and Traumas in the Twentieth Century* (Cambridge, Mass.: Harvard University Press, 2002). Michael Levine and Bella Brodzki have edited an excellent collection on this topic as it was opened up by Felman's book; see "Trials of Trauma," special issue, *Comparative Literature Studies* 48, no. 2 (2011). Although the Dorfman play does not involve an actual trial, it does involve a kind of staged trial that raises issues related to the use of trials in other transitional states. On this issue see, among others, Mark Osiel, *Mass Atrocity, Collective Memory, and the Law* (New Brunswick, N.J.: Transaction Publishers, 1997).

24. For a variety of perspectives on the play, see Robert F. Barsky, "Outsider Law in Literature: Construction and Representation in *Death and the Maiden*," *SubStance*, no. 84 (1997): 66–89; Pércio B. de Castro, "*La muerte y la doncella ¿De quién son las bolas? Opresor, oprimido y viceversa,*" *Revista Chilena de Literatura*, no. 52 (April 1998): 61–67; David Luban, "Essay: On Dorfman's *Death and the Maiden*," *Yale Journal of Law & the Humanities* (Winter 1998); Sophia A. McClennan, *Ariel Dorfman: An Aesthetics of Hope* (Durham, N.C.: Duke University Press, 2010), esp. 160–76; Roberto A. Morace, "The Life and Times of *Death and the Maiden*," *Texas Studies in Literature and Language* 42, no. 2 (2000): 135–53; Amy Novak, "Gendering Trauma: Ariel Dorfman's Narratives of Crisis and Reconciliation," *Critique: Studies in Contemporary Fiction* 48, no. 3 (2007): 295–317; Carolyn Pinet, "Retrieving the Disappeared Text: Women, Chaos, and Change in Argentina and Chile after the Dirty Wars," *Hispanic Journal* 18, no. 1 (1997): 89–108; Kimberly Rostan, "Sweet Are the Uses of Tragedy: *Death and the Maiden*'s 'Almost Aristotelian' Testimony," *Atenea: A Bilingual Journal of the Humanities and Social Sciences* 25, no. 2 (December 2005): 9–24. There are

many apparently simple oppositions set up in the play (e.g., seeing and hearing, man and woman) that the play puts into question—at least in its Spanish version or in the relation between its Spanish and English versions.

25. It should be noted, also, that Roberto uses the word "roles" in relation to the word "interrogation" in the Spanish (*MD*, 62), thus associating performance and torture.

26. Thus music is both the referent and its reiteration here, or rather it is the erasure of the referent carried on in the performance. To the extent that Paulina misses the moment when she has become inscribed in Roberto's performance, the music becomes the reenactment of that missed moment.

27. From the beginning of the play, Gerardo has attempted to cut Paulina off when she begins to speak, and she indicates at one point that Gerardo has not asked about the specifics of her experience under torture.

28. Perhaps the music might be thought of, here, in the context of what Jean-Francois Lyotard calls the "*differend*." See Jean-Francois Lyotard, *The Differend: Phrases in Dispute* (Minneapolis: University of Minnesota Press, 1989).

29. It might be interesting to consider "disappearing" as a form of the "modern lie" that partakes both in what Hannah Arendt called "terror" (in the totalitarian context) and "image-making" (in the postwar nontotalitarian context).

30. A very useful article on music in the play is David Schroeder, "Dorfman, Schubert, and *Death and the Maiden*," *Comparative Literature and Culture* 9, no.1 (March 2007). One might recall as well George Steiner's well-known remark about those who could "play and sing Schubert in the evening and torture in the morning": "The Muses' Farewell," *Salmagundi* 135–36 (Summer–Fall 2002): 150. Music was also used to cover up the screams of torture victims during the Dirty War, a more literal "hiding" of the torture but not the kind of disappearing of the torture with which Dorfman primarily engages in his text.

31. It is important to reiterate that the music is not only associated with torture but constitutes it (and also figures it in the play). And this torture consists also in the erasure of itself as evidence (the inability to use the music or its effects as a means of evidence).

32. The emphasis on sound (voice and music) requires us to rethink the nature of sound and of listening. The apparent opposition between seeing and hearing in the play, associated with the impasse between the two notions of justice offered by Gerardo and Paulina, must be rethought in terms of the nature of the music, and, in particular, the nature of this quartet by Schubert, as I have analyzed it later in this chapter.

I have not considered the role of the doctor here; on doctors and torture, see, for example, Robert Jay Lifton, *The Nazi Doctors: Medical Killing and the Psychology of Genocide* (New York: Basic Books, 2000); he has also written on this topic in relation to doctors at Guantanamo in "Doctors and Torture," *New England Journal of Medicine* 351 (July 2004): 415–41.

33. It is interesting to note that the full Spanish phrase for "my role, the role

of good guy, as they call it" is "*al rol que me tocaba hacer, el rol del bueno, que le dicen*," which includes the verb *tocar*, though here used in a grammatical construction to indicate that Roberto was forced or pressed to play the role by others (something like "the role I had to play"). The self-deceptive aspect of Roberto's language is evident here.

34. Critics have noted the element of betrayal in the use of the music. I am interested in the specific form of turning life or listening itself into a kind of betrayal, that is, an unwitting performance of a role scripted by another. On betrayal trauma in general, see Jennifer J. Freyd, *Betrayal Trauma: The Logic of Forgetting Childhood Abuse* (Cambridge, Mass.: Harvard University Press, 1998).

35. Roberto does, at one point, acknowledge the "brutality" that has overtaken him, but he frames his discourse with the excuse of saving the prisoners. Of course later he will claim that the entire confession was staged.

36. For the sense in which Paulina is "played" like an instrument, one might recall the use of these terms in another highly self-reflexive play, Shakespeare's *Hamlet*, in which Hamlet says to Guildenstern, "Well, playing the recorder should be easy, as you seem to play me like a pipe pretty well, you liar."

37. We might recall Videla's use of language, here, reflected in Roberto's use of the phrase "the real real truth" (*la verdad la verdad*). (Roberto is also, as noted above, the first person, in his encounter with Gerardo, to raise the question of truth—in relation to the reason for his appearance at the house in the middle of the night). Roberto, too, uses a kind of human rights discourse that is (self-)deceiving in this "confession" on the tape: "The real real truth, it was for humanitarian reasons . . . they still have the right to some medical attention."

38. The use of verbal repetition throughout the play has been noted by various critics. It is important to read this repetition, I am suggesting, in relation to the status of repetition involved in recording.

39. It is interesting that Paulina claims she wants the testimony of Roberto, though she wants it only for herself. One of the problems of the testimony acted out in the play is the purely personal dimension of the performance. The Chilean commission also kept the persecutors' names secret and did not create a public performance, of sorts, as did the South African Truth and Reconciliation Commission. On notions of performance in the latter, see Catherine M. Cole, *Performing South Africa's Truth Commission: Stages of Transition* (Bloomington: Indiana University Press, 2010).

40. The word is also linked to the word for "grave," thus also binding music, inscription, and death.

41. The nature of activity and passivity is thus transferred to the ear from the more obvious context of action throughout the play. I would like to thank Sylvia Chong for noting the relation between the recorder and the ear.

42. It should be noted that the use of *tocar* for the pressing of the buttons on the recorder occurs only when Paulina, and not Gerardo, presses the buttons, thus confirming the sense that the problem of performance in relation to music and its

association with the verb *tocar* is sustained rigorously through the play. This is particularly interesting since Ariel Dorfman removed from the English version at least one instance of the use of *tocar*—and made no apparent attempt to translate into English its resonance in Spanish—thus indicating that he was working (or the language was working) unconsciously in his text.

43. The hearing/listening of Paulina (and perhaps of the audience) thus becomes a kind of living-on or deathly survival. We might think, here, of the dynamics of "archive fever," in Derrida's formulation, which pass on what is also passed over or erased. See Jacques Derrida, *Mal d'Archive: Une impression freudienne* (Paris: Galilée, 1995); English translations from Jacques Derrida, *Archive Fever: A Freudian Impression*, trans. Eric Prenowitz (Chicago: University of Chicago Press, 1995). Paulina's question about the "originality" of the tape of the *Death and the Maiden* quartet that she has found in Roberto's car also points to a question concerning the search for the true first marking, the desire to retrieve the event in its purity and to archive it as such.

44. Roberto's line also echoes Gerardo's earlier question to Paulina in act 2.

45. Claus Westermann, *Genesis 1–11: A Continental Commentary* (Minneapolis, Minn.: Fortress Press, 1994). It would be interesting to consider the "primal" nature of this scene in relation to the law.

46. Paulina has spoken earlier about her desire to feel Gerardo making love to her again without the intrusion of this past, thus suggesting that for her the lovemaking has involved, for her, a problem with his touch.

47. One might also consider the nature of performance in relation to the movement from (silent, or mute—simply read) stage directions to performance, as well as the performance involved in translation. For a wonderful essay on the movement from text to performance, see Joseph Roach, "Performance: The Blunders of Orpheus," in "Literary Criticism for the Twenty-First Century," ed. Cathy Caruth and Jonathan Culler, special issue, *PMLA* 125, no. 4 (October 2010): 1078–87. On the problem of translation, see Ariel Dorfman, *Feeding on Dreams: Confessions of an Unrepentant Exile* (New York: Houghton Mifflin Harcourt, 2011).

48. One of the interesting motifs in this play that I do not have space to consider here is the figure of moonlight, which becomes particularly prominent in the English version of the play, and especially in relation to the tape recorder.

49. See Roberto's reading aloud of his confession in act 3 (*DM*, 58–60).

50. The "performance" of music in the last act is particularly complex; the stage directions indicate that the music is to be played but we do not see the musicians, and in the English they are explicitly referred to as "imaginary," just as the audience for the music is "invisible." This is presumably the moment when the play has reached the height of self-reflexivity with the mirror, but it is also a highly figurative moment that puts into question the clarity of the reflection as a reflection (we might think of the faces in the mirror coming before the audience and actors as, perhaps, giving us the faces of the disappeared, as the placards of the

Mothers of the Plaza de Mayo did—hence faces that are also prosopopoeic figures of absence or death as much as representations of living, present people). Diana Fuss has suggested to me that we might think of the mirror at this point in the play in terms of the footnote in *Beyond the Pleasure Principle* in which Freud describes the child (of the *fort/da* game) making himself appear and disappear in a mirror. The emphasis on marking in the play, as well as the introduction of these prosopopoeic figures in the Claudius poem that Schubert sets to music, and possibly in the use of the mirror, suggest that not only the notion of hearing but also of seeing may not necessarily be aligned, in this play, with sensory models of perception. This is significant because the model of listening (and perhaps seeing) that is associated with interpreting marks or reading figures might make it possible to think of a mode of receiving the testimony of various kinds of performance in a manner that does not simply repeat the traumatizing imposition of sound in the torture, or the implicit perversion of pleasure in Roberto's use of music as he inflicts pain. I would also like to note that it is impossible to decide what kind of "performance" is involved here (for example, which use of the verb *tocar* in the last words, to*ca y toca y toca*): Is this "performing" as on an instrument, or "playing" as on a tape?

51. I would like to thank Avery Slater for her brilliant remarks concerning the strange way in which the repeated note of "Death" in the Schubert song may both require and resist differentiation.

Chapter Five: Psychoanalysis in the Ashes of History

1. Wilhelm Jensen, *Gradiva: A Pompeiian Fantasy*, trans. Helen M. Downey, reprinted in *Delusion and Dream: An Interpretation in the Light of Psychoanalysis of "Gradiva," a Novel by Wilhelm Jensen* (New York: New Republic, 1927). Hereafter cited as *G*. I would like to thank Armando Mastrogiovanni for research assistance related to this chapter.

2. Jacques Derrida, *Mal d'Archive: Une impression freudienne* (Paris: Galilée, 1995); English translations from Jacques Derrida, *Archive Fever: A Freudian Impression*, trans. Eric Prenowitz (Chicago: University of Chicago Press, 1995). Hereafter cited as *MdA* and *AF*.

3. Jacques Derrida, *Mal d'Archive*, "Prière d'insérer," 1; this insert is not included in the English translation. Hereafter cited as PI. The translation is my own.

4. On the archaeological metaphor in Freud, see Richard H. Armstrong, "The Archaeology of Freud's Archaeology: Recent Work in the History of Psychoanalysis," *International Review of Modernism* 3, no. 1 (1999): 16–20; Suzanne Cassirer Bernfeld, "Freud and Archaeology," *American Imago* 8 (1951): 107–28; Sabine Hake, "Saxe Loquuntur: Freud's Archaeology of the Text," *boundary* 2 20, no. 1 (1993): 146–73; Donald Kuspit, "A Mighty Metaphor: The Analogy of Archaeology and Psychoanalysis," in *Sigmund Freud and Art: His Personal Collection of Antiquities*, ed. Lynn Gamwell and Richard Wells, 133–51 (London: Thames and Hudson, 1989); Dragan Kujundžic, "Archigraphia: On the Future of Testimony

and the Archive to Come," *Discourse* 25, nos. 1–2 (Winter–Spring 2004): 166–88; Steen F. Larsen, "Remembering and the Archaeology Metaphor," *Metaphor and Symbol* 2, no. 3 (September 1987): 187–99; Kenneth Reinhard, "The Freudian Things: Construction and the Archaeological Metaphor," in *Excavations and Their Objects: Freud's Collection of Antiquity*, ed. Stephen Barker (Albany: State University of New York Press, 1996); Peter Rudnytsky, "Freud's Pompeian Fantasy," in *Reading Freud's Reading*, ed. Sander Gilman (New York: New York University Press, 1995); Donald P. Spence, *The Freudian Metaphor: Toward Paradigm Change in Psychoanalysis* (New York: W. W. Norton, 1987); Christfried Tögel, *Berggasse—Pompeji und Zurück: Sigmund Freuds Reisen in die Vergangenheit* (Tübingen: Edition Diskord, 1989).

5. Jacques Lacan, "Tuché and Automaton," in *The Four Fundamental Concepts of Psychoanalysis: Book XI of the Seminar of Jacques Lacan* (New York: W. W. Norton, 1998), 54.

6. Derrida analyzes this structure of the memory trace in the *Project* in "Freud and the Scene of Writing." See Jacques Derrida, "Freud and the Scene of Writing," in *Writing and Difference*, trans. Alan Bass (Chicago: University of Chicago Press, 1978), 203. Alan Bass has a good summary of the first section of Derrida's essay in *Interpretation and Difference: The Strangeness of Care* (Stanford: Stanford University Press, 2006). On *Archive Fever*, see also Carolyn Steedman, *Dust* (Manchester: Manchester University Press 2001).

7. Freud thus allows us to think of the potential historicity of the concept of *Nachträglichkeit*. On the development of this concept, see also Jean Laplanche, *Problématiques VI: L'Après-coup* (Paris: Presses Universitaires de France, 2006). Cynthia Chase offers an exceptional reading of the relation between this concept and the writing of Freud's theory in his incorporation of the Oedipus tragedy in *The Interpretation of Dreams* in "Oedipal Textuality," in her *Decomposing Figures: Rhetorical Readings in the Romantic Tradition* (Baltimore: Johns Hopkins University Press, 1986).

8. See Cathy Caruth, *Unclaimed Experience: Trauma, Narrative and History* (Baltimore: Johns Hopkins University Press, 1996), chap. 3, "Traumatic Departures: Survival and History in Freud."

9. Robert Jay Lifton, "Survivor Experience and Traumatic Syndrome," in his *The Broken Connection: On Death and the Continuity of Life* (New York: Basic Books, 1979). See also Cathy Caruth, "An Interview with Robert Jay Lifton" in *Trauma: Explorations in Memory*, ed. Cathy Caruth (Baltimore: Johns Hopkins University Press, 1995).

10. Yosef Hayim Yerushalmi, *Freud's Moses: Judaism Terminable and Interminable* (New Haven: Yale University Press, 1991).

11. On Freud's reading of Jensen's *Gradiva*, see Mary Bergstein, "Gradiva Medica: Freud's Model Female Analyst as Lizard-Slayer," *American Imago* 60, no. 3 (2003): 285–301; Eric Downing, "Archaeology, Psychoanalysis, and Bildung

in Freud and Wilhelm Jensen's *Gradiva*," in his *After Images: Photography, Archaeology, and Psychoanalysis and the Tradition of Bildung* (Detroit: Wayne State University Press, 2006); Sander L. Gilman, *Freud, Race, and Gender* (Princeton: Princeton University Press, 1993); Neil Hertz, foreword to *Sigmund Freud: Writings on Art and Literature* (Stanford: Stanford University Press, 1997); Mary Jacobus, *Reading Woman: Essays in Feminist Criticism* (New York: Columbia University Press, 1986); Barbara Johnson, *Moses and Multiculturalism* (Berkeley: University of California Press, 2010); Sarah Kofman, *Freud and Fiction* (Cambridge: Polity Press, 1991); Leonard Lawlor, "Memory Becomes Elektra," *Review of Politics* 60, no. 4 (1998): 796–8; Lis Møller, *The Freudian Reading: Analytical and Fictional Constructions* (Philadelphia: University of Pennsylvania Press, 1991); Nicholas Rand and Maria Torok, "A Case Study in Literary Psychoanalysis: Jensen's *Gradiva*," in Rand and Torok, *Questions for Freud: The Secret History of Psychoanalysis* (Cambridge: Harvard University Press, 1997); Michael Rohrwasser, Gisela Steinlechner, Juliane Vogel, and Christiane Zintzen, *Freuds pomejanische Muse: Beiträge zu Wilhelm Jensens Novelle "Gradiva"* (Vienna: Sonderzahl, 1996). On Derrida and the figure of ash, see also David Krell, *The Purest of Bastards: Works of Mourning, Art, and Affirmation in the Thought of Jacques Derrida* (University Park: Penn State University Press, 2000).

12. This is the Strachey translation edited by Neil Hertz, in *Sigmund Freud: Writings on Art and Literature* (Stanford: Stanford University Press, 1997), 35 (translation modified). Hertz offers a brilliant reading of art, immobilization, and sculpture—which touches on Freud's *Gradiva* essay—in his foreword to this book.

13. Perhaps an echo of "*verweile doch, du bist so schön*," from Goethe's *Faust*.

14. It is interesting to recall Giuseppe Fiorelli's work at the site of Pompeii in the nineteenth century, drilling holes in the tephra, sending plaster down into the cavities created by the incinerated bodies and bringing up their forms. The volcano, in the context of Derrida's reading of Freud's interpretation of Jensen, becomes something of a "writing machine," in the sense in which Derrida refers to it in "Freud and the Scene of Writing." Of course the total incineration of bodies, understood in the context of the total destruction of the archive, would leave no forms or traces behind.

The full range of meanings of "impression," which I have not discussed in this chapter, calls for its own reading in relation to other figures that are prominent in Derrida's reading of Jensen and Freud, as Sam Weber pointed out in an outstanding (unpublished) response to an earlier version of this chapter. Two excellent, relatively recent works, which focus on different aspects of Derrida's relation to, and citation of, Jensen's *Gradiva* in various texts, are Daniel Orrells, "Derrida's Impression of *Gradiva*: *Archive Fever* and Antiquity," in *Derrida and Antiquity*, ed. Miriam Leonard (Oxford: Oxford University Press, 2010), and Michael Naas, *Miracle and Machine: Jacques Derrida and the Two Sources of Religion, Science, and the Media* (New York: Fordham University Press, 2012).

15. It is intriguing to note that the word in German is not "foot-prints" but "toe-prints," which is often lost in translation, including Derrida's French. As Cynthia Chase pointed out to me, the toe takes on the form of a whole—the foot—as it passes into translation.

16. Jacques Derrida, *Cinders*, trans. Ned Lukacher (Lincoln: University of Nebraska Press, 1991), 59. For Derrida's comments on trauma and the future, see Giovanna Borradori, "Autoimmunity: Real and Symbolic Suicides—A Dialogue with Jacques Derrida," in Giovanna Borradori, *Philosophy in a Time of Terror: Dialogues with Jürgen Habermas and Jacques Derrida* (Chicago: University of Chicago Press, 2004).

It should be noted that the impressions of the Gradiva figure associated with the bas-relief in this story are not precisely the same as those associated with ancient sculpture, as the bas-relief is a modern copy (of a Roman copy of a Greek bas-relief) that is purchased by Hanold as something like a souvenir. And of course Jensen and Freud purchased their own copies, as did a variety of others, following Freud. The multiplication of impressions, or copies, of the bas-relief thus may perhaps be thought in relation to the kind of replication discussed by Walter Benjamin in "The Work of Art in the Age of its Technical Reproducibility." Indeed, the Jensen novella, with its phantasm and its antiquity, at first reads a bit like a nineteenth-century literary story, but upon closer inspection may come across more like a cheap reproduction of such a story, which is perhaps why Freud would say, at one point after he had published his essay, that the novella was not a great work of art (a point we might wish to consider in relation to the theme of reproducibility rather than to a simple aesthetic judgment).

17. Jacques Derrida, "Poetics and Politics of Witnessing," in *Sovereignties in Question: The Poetics of Paul Celan*, ed. Thomas Dutoit and Outi Pasanen (New York: Fordham University Press, 2005).

18. Jacques Derrida and Elisabeth Weber, "Passages—From Traumatism to Promise," in *Points . . . Interviews, 1974–1994*, ed. Elisabeth Weber (Stanford: Stanford University Press, 1995).

19. See also Jacques Derrida, "No Apocalypse, Not Now (full speed ahead, seven missiles, seven missives)," trans. Catherine Porter and Philip Lewis, *Diacritics* (Summer 1984).

20. Elaine Caruth, Ph.D., personal communication.

21. Walter Benjamin, "Theses on the Philosophy of History," in *Illuminations: Essays and Reflections*, ed. Hannah Arendt (New York: Schocken 1969), 264.

22. Francoise Davoine, "The Characters of Madness in the Talking Cure," *Psychoanalytic Dialogues* 17, no. 5 (September 2007): 627–38.

23. In *Beyond the Pleasure Principle*, Freud talks a bit about figures, about the figurative language necessary to articulate the speculative concept of the death drive, and of the colorings of Eros entangled with the muteness of the drive to death. Eros, here, is not pleasure, but rather the love story that, for Norbert Hanold, is the search for the origins of Gradiva in her traces, and, for Freud, the

compulsive desire for a return to the origin, an archival desire, a desire for witness and a desire that, itself, attempts to bear witness.

24. See also Derrida, "No Apocalypse, Not Now": "The hypothesis of this total destruction watches over deconstruction, it guides its footsteps."

25. Toni Morrison, *A Mercy* (New York: Vintage, 2006), 188.

claim (*cont.*)
    to a new mode of survival, xi; to
        property, 18–19, 21–22, 25–28, 32;
        to survival, xi, 27; and witness, 9, 32
Claudius, Matthias, "Death and the
    Maiden," 72–73
Cleary, Edward L., 109n6
Cold War, 48
Cole, Catherine M., 115n39
Collins, Cath, 111n10
communism, 46, 47, 48
compromise, 19, 26–28, 30–35,
    101nn9–10
confession, 54, 60–61, 64–66, 68–70, 72
consciousness: disappearance from, x,
    57; of the law, 22; limits of, ix–x,
    77–78, 80, 86; origins of, 5–9, 80,
    94–95n10
creative act (creation), 4, 8–9, 13, 52,
    53, 71, 83, 87; and creativity, 4, 9, 12,
    13, 17, 26, 95–96n13; of the game,
    15, 94n9; of history, 9, 29, 40, 45, 78;
    of the image, 45–49; of invention,
    4–5; and language, 9, 15–16; of the
    lie, 42–43, 46; of life, 5; and listening,
    63; of new events, x, 77; of a new
    kind of fact, 50; of parting, 16–17;
    and politics, 33, 39–41, 56; and
    re-creation, 12, 28, 60; and war,
    45–47; of witness, 5, 9, 12–14. *See
    also under* death drive

Davoine, Francoise, 90
death, 5–14, 16, 21–25, 27, 29, 31, 57,
    63, 67, 73, 78, 96n14; penalty, 60;
    sentence, 71; and survival, xii, 11,
    18–19, 27, 33–34, 116n43. *See also
    under* witness
death drive, xi, 5–6, 8, 9, 15, 17, 32,
    78, 79, 95–96nn12–13, 98n22,
    99nn26–27; as creative act, 16
de Castro, Pércio B., 113n24
deception. *See* lie
*Declaration of the Rights of Man and
    Citizen of 1789*, 20, 28
defactualization, 47–49
deferral, 6, 15, 80–81, 83, 85, 87. *See
    also* Nachträglichkeit
dehumanization, 25

de Man, Paul, 108n15
democracy, x, 59, 61; return to, 54, 55,
    56, 58, 59, 60, 109n5
departure, 14–16; and return, 4, 14–15,
    80–81, 87, 94n7, 97n19. *See also
    fort/da*
de Preau, Charles Theodore Beauvais,
    100n5
Derrida, Jacques, xi, 87, 92; *Archive
    Fever*, 75–84, 88–89, 116n42;
    "Autoimmunity, Real and Symbolic
    Suicides," 120n16; *Cinders*, 87;
    "Declarations of Independence,"
    103n14, 106n25; "Freud and the
    Scene of Writing," 118n6, 119n14;
    "History of the Lie, Prolegomena,"
    107n7; "Now Apocalypse, Not Now,"
    120n19, 121n24; "Passages—From
    Traumatism to Promise," 87; "Poetics
    and Politics of Witnessing," 87; "To
    Speculate—on 'Freud'," 93n3, 96n14,
    98n21, 98n25
Diaz, Nicole, 111n11
dictatorship, x, 54, 60
disappearance, 56–57, 65, 69, 71, 72,
    90; of disappearance, 57; of the event,
    57, 61, 77; and evidence, 68, 114n31;
    of facts, 57; of history, ix–xi, 41, 55,
    61–62, 70–71, 90; under Pinochet, 54,
    55, 56–57, 108n2; and return, ix–x,
    55–58, 62, 67, 73–74. *See also* erasure
    and under memory; performance;
    repetition
Dorfman, Ariel, x, xi, 92; *Death and
    the Maiden*, 54–56, 58–74, 108n1,
    116n47
Downing, Eric, 118n11
dreams, 3–6, 8, 24, 75–76, 78, 82,
    84–87, 89–90, 91
Duncan, Ted, 97n15
Duras, Marguerite (and Alain Resnais),
    Hiroshima mon amour, 95–96n13

Ellsberg, Daniel, 44, 52–53, 107n11
end, after the, 88, 91–92
Ensalaco, Mark, 109n6
erasure, 22, 69, 71, 84–87; and the
    bomb, 50–51; and history, 50–52,
    75–81, 87; and the image, 48–50; of

reality (*cont.*)
  referent, 63; ungraspable, 6; of war, 4,
    22–23, 44. *See also under* reenactment
reclaiming. *See* claim
Reinhard, Kenneth, 118n4
reenactment: of an event, 57–58, 65;
    of a performance, 57, 60–61, 67, 71;
    of reality, 4; of torture, 66–67; of
    trauma, 55, 58
referent, 57, 59, 63, 71, 88
repetition, 43, 45, 87, 105n23; in
    Beyond the Pleasure Principle, ix,
    3–10, 13–17, 57, 78–81; and creation,
    4–5, 8, 15, 33, 60; of disappearance,
    x, 57, 62; of erasure, 51, 78–81, 84,
    86–87; of explosion, 50–52; in Freud's
    reading of Jensen, 83–87, 90; and
    history, 18, 32, 62, 78–80; of the
    incomprehensible or new, 7, 9, 32,
    73, 87, 89, 92, 104n21; and law, 18,
    32–33; and the modern lie, 45; as
    origin, 8–9, 80; and psychoanalysis,
    ix, 3, 7, 15, 77–81, 86; and recording,
    59–62, 64–65, 67–70, 72, 115n38;
    and trauma, 3–4, 6–8, 15–17, 24–25,
    78–79, 81, 87. *See also under* event,
    the; performance
representation, 4, 30, 40, 69, 78
repression, ix, 22, 75, 76, 77, 78, 79,
    82, 85, 86
Resnais, Alain. *See* Duras, Marguerite
Restoration France, 18, 20, 21, 27, 28,
    30, 32
retribution, 25–26, 31, 33, 61, 70
return, 55–59, 63–64, 85–86; and death
    or the dead, 7, 12–13, 15, 18–25, 29,
    31, 78; to the dream, 90; and history,
    3, 20–21, 24, 25; and memory, xi, 4,
    21, 79, 83–84; to the origin, 77–78,
    80, 83, 120–21n23; to the past, 21,
    27, 59–61, 78, 87, 91; to Pompeii,
    82–83, 88–89, 91; and trauma, 23–25,
    80, 87; as unrecognizable, 87, 92. *See
    also* democracy: return to; departure:
    and return; disappearance: and return;
    property: restitution or return of;
    repetition
revenge. *See* retribution

rights, 25, 61; human rights, 28, 55–56,
    67, 70, 109n5; the rightless, 57,
    104n20. *See also* claim; law; property
Roach, Joseph, 116n47
Rohrwasser, Michael, 119n11
Roosevelt, Franklin Delano, 47
Rostan, Kimberly, 113n24
Rudnytsky, Peter, 118n4

Santner, Eric L., 93n3
Sarat, Austin, 109n5
Schroeder, David, 114n30
Schubert, Franz, *Death and the Maiden*,
    54–68, 71–73, 114n30
Schwab, Gabriele, 110n9
secret, ix, 29, 30, 31, 44, 52, 53, 59,
    84
seduction, 66
Shapiro, Martin, 101n9
shock. *See* surprise
silence, 23, 32, 39, 79, 88
singularity, 19, 67, 75, 76, 79, 83, 84,
    86, 87, 88
Sivert, Eileen B., 104n17
Sledziewski, Elisabeth, 101–2n10,
    103n12
soldier(s). *See* French Revolution;
    World War I; World War II
Soviet Union, 40, 47
Spence, Donald P., 118n4
Steedman, Carolyn, 118n4
Steiner, George, 114n30
surprise, 3–4, 5–6, 9, 11, 12, 18, 44,
    54, 62, 77–80, 82, 91, 95n11
survival, 32, 45, 67, 70, 78, 81,
    95–96n13; of historical disappear-
    ance, xi; and missed experience, 6;
    and the name, 34; new kind of, xi,
    16–17. *See also under* claim; death;
    experience; future; history; language;
    witness

Taylor, Diana, 112n16
Teitel, Ruth G., 109n5
testimony, 9, 53, 55, 58, 66–70, 84.
    See also witness
Thanatos. *See* death drive; erasure;
    repetition

Thomas, Stephen B., 97n15
Tögel, Christfried, 118n4
Torok, Maria, 119n11
torture, 54–67, 69–72. *See also under* reenactment
totalitarianism, 41, 43, 50–51
touch, 70–74
trace, 50, 62, 82–87, 89–90; in ashes, 75, 82–84, 86–87, 91–92; and erasure, 52, 79, 87; and figure, 52, 53. *See also under* memory
trauma, 58, 80–81, 91, 94–95nn10–11, 95–96nn13–14; century of, 16; theory of, xii, 4–5, 7–8, 15–17, 57; and traumatized child, 10; and traumatic dreams, 3, 6, 8, 86; and traumatic encounter, 5–6; and traumatic future, 81, 87; and traumatic loss, ix; and traumatic past, 19, 21; and traumatic struggles, x. *See also* survival
trial, 19, 54, 55, 58, 60–61, 64, 67, 109n4
Trotsky, Leon, 40
Truman, Harry S, 47, 49
truth, 53, 54–55, 59, 61, 72; commission, 54, 55, 59, 64, 67 (*see also* National Commission on Truth and Reconciliation); factual, 40–41; historical, 83; inaccessibility of, 64; possibility of, 58–59; and truth-telling, 41–42, 53. *See also under* exclusion; law; performance

unconscious, the, 3, 6, 7, 9, 22, 57, 59, 60, 61, 73, 76, 77, 78, 82, 83, 84, 90, 91

van der Kolk, Bessel A., 95n10
vengeance. *See* retribution
Vesuvius, xi, 75, 85, 88, 91
Videla, Rafael, 56–57, 115n37

Vietnam War, 44–49, 52–53
violence, 39, 43–44, 50, 53, 63; urban, 10
voice, 54, 59, 60, 65–69, 72–73

war. *See* Eylau, battle of; French Revolution; Vietnam War; World War I; World War II
Weber, Samuel, 93n3, 119n14
Weimar Republic, 40
Weissbrodt, David, 110n6
Westermann, Claus, 70
Whitehead, Ann, 98–99n25
Winnicott, D. W., 99n27
wish-fulfillment, 3–4, 85–86, 93n2
witness: to death, 3–7, 9–10, 13–14, 16, 24; and defactualization, 40, 48, 53; to disappearing history, xi, 67; of history, xi, 33–34, 39, 48, 52–53, 76, 79–81, 91; of modern lie, 52–53; new kind of, 4–5, 13, 52–53, 90; of a new kind of event, 77–78, 80, 89, 91–92; and parting, 9, 11, 13–14; of past and future, xi, 9–10, 35, 91–92; of repetition, 9; strange, 87–88; to suffering (*mal*), 75; of survival, 7, 24, 32, 34, 81; to the unexperienced, 6. *See also under* ash; claim; creative act; erasure; law; memory; psychoanalysis
World War I, ix, 3, 10, 16, 40, 41, 43, 51, 53, 57, 78, 81
World War II, 40, 50, 51, 53
Wright, Thomas C., 110n6
writing, xi, 69, 75; in ashes, 89; buried, 77; burning, 87, 90; of a new origination of thought, 88; rewriting, 41–43. *See also* inscription

Yerushalmi, Yosef Hayim, *Freud's Moses, Psychoanalysis Terminable and Interminable*, 81, 89